Magna Carta

THE TAX REVOLT THAT
GAVE US LIBERTY

ALSO FROM
THE INSTITUTE OF PUBLIC AFFAIRS

Climate Change:
The Facts
(2015)
edited by Alan Moran
with contributions from
John Abbot & Jennifer Marohasy
Andrew Bolt ~ Robert M Carter
Rupert Darwall ~ James Delingpole
Christopher Essex ~ Stewart W Franks
Kesten C Green & J Scott Armstrong
Donna Laframboise ~ Nigel Lawson
Bernie Lewin ~ Richard S Lindzen
Ross McKitrick ~ Alan Moran
Patrick J Michaels ~ Joanne Nova
Garth W Paltridge ~ Ian Plimer
Willie Soon ~ Mark Steyn
and Anthony Watts

~

ALSO BY MARK STEYN

Lights Out:
Islam, Free Speech And The Twilight Of The West
(2009)

MAGNA CARTA

THE TAX REVOLT THAT GAVE US LIBERTY

Chris Berg and John Roskam
with Stephanie Forrest

foreword by Mark Steyn

STOCKADE
BOOKS

First published by the Institute of Public Affairs, Melbourne, Victoria

Published in 2015 by
Stockade Books
Box 30, Woodsville, New Hampshire 03785

Printed and bound in the Province of Québec, Canada

ISBN 978-0-9863983-7-7

At Runnymede, at Runnymede,
What say the reeds at Runnymede?
The lissom reeds that give and take,
That bend so far, but never break,
They keep the sleepy Thames awake
With tales of John at Runnymede.

At Runnymede, at Runnymede,
Oh, hear the reeds at Runnymede:
You musn't sell, delay, deny,
A freeman's right or liberty.
It wakes the stubborn Englishry,
We saw 'em roused at Runnymede!

RUDYARD KIPLING

CHRIS BERG is a Senior Fellow with the Institute of Public Affairs. He is author of *Liberty, Equality & Democracy*, *In Defence of Freedom of Speech*, and *The Growth of Australia's Regulatory State*.

JOHN ROSKAM is Executive Director of the Institute of Public Affairs. He is co-editor of *100 Great Books of Liberty* and co-author of *Australia's Education Choices*.

STEPHANIE FORREST is a Research Scholar at the Institute of Public Affairs and author of *Australia's British Heritage* (forthcoming).

MARK STEYN is the international bestselling author of *America Alone*, *After America* and *The [Un]documented Mark Steyn*.

*The Institute of Public Affairs gratefully acknowledges
the encouragement and support of Mr Chris Abbott
for the production of this work.*

CONTENTS

FOREWORD
by Mark Steyn

The field where liberty was sown

EIGHT CENTURIES ago, a king found himself in a muddy field on the River Thames near Windsor Castle. It's not generally a good sign when a king finds himself in a field, but it went better for King John than it did for Richard III. Under His Majesty's nose and awaiting his seal was the great foundational document of individual liberty.

The world has come a long way since Magna Carta, and not always for the best. A couple of years back, testifying to the House of Commons in Ottawa about the iniquities of Canada's (now repealed) censorship law, I said the following:

Section 13 is at odds with this country's entire legal inheritance, stretching back to Magna Carta. Back then, if

i

you recall, in 1215, human rights meant that the King could be restrained by his subjects. Eight hundred years later, Canada's pseudo-human rights apparatchiks of the commission have entirely inverted that proposition, and human rights now mean that the subjects get restrained by the Crown in the cause of so-called collective rights that can be regulated only by the state.

I liked it better the old way. Real rights are like Magna Carta: restraints on state power. Too many people today understand the word "rights" to mean baubles and trinkets a gracious sovereign bestows on his subjects - "free" health care, "free" community college, "safe spaces" from anyone saying anything beastly to them - all of which require a massive, coercive state regulatory regime to enforce.

But, to give it its full name, Magna Carta *Libertatum* (my italics - I don't think they had 'em back then) gets it the right way round. It was in some respects a happy accident. In 1215, a bunch of chippy barons were getting fed up with King John. In those days, in such circumstances, the malcontents would usually replace the sovereign with a pliable prince who'd be more attentive to their grievances. But, having no such prince to hand, the barons were forced to be more inventive, and so they wound up replacing the King with an idea, and the most important idea of all - that even the King is subject to the law; that government requires consent.

On this 800th anniversary, that's a lesson worth re-learning. Restraints on state power are increasingly unfashionable among the heirs to Magna Carta: in America, King Barack decides when he wakes up of a morning what clauses of Obamacare or US immigration law he's willing to observe or waive according to royal whim; his heir presumptive, Queen Hillary, operates on the principle that laws are for the other 300 million Americans, not her. In the birthplace of Magna Carta, a few miles from that meadow at Runnymede David Cameron's constabulary leans on newsagents to cough up the names and addresses of troublesome citizens who've committed the crime of purchasing *Charlie Hebdo*.

The symbolism was almost too perfect when Mr Cameron went on TV with David Letterman, and was obliged to admit that he had no idea what the words "Magna Carta" meant. Magna Carta Libertatum: The Great Charter of Liberties. I'm happy to say Mr Cameron's Commonwealth cousins across the Atlantic in Ottawa are more on top of things: One of the modestly heartening innovations of Stephen Harper's ministry is that, when immigrants to Canada take the oath of allegiance, they're now given among other things their own personal copy of Magna Carta.

Why? Because everything flows therefrom - from England's Glorious Revolution to the US Constitution and beyond. It's part of the reason why the English-speaking world, in contrast to Continental Europe, has managed to sustain its freedoms across the generations - at least until now. As my compatriot John Robson, announcing his own forthcoming documentary on Magna Carta, put it:

> *All the rights we cherish, from due process of law to elected representatives, trace back to it. It has been assailed time and again and always defended. It's why we have rights today. But that story needs to be told again and again or it will be lost and with it our freedom.*

Security of the person, property rights, religious freedom, due process... The core animating principles of modern free societies began in that muddy field at Runnymede eight centuries ago.

Sometimes - often - a free people can lose the inclination of liberty and accept the provocations of the state no matter how absurd. In 2013, due to a stand-off between the Republicans and Democrats over federal funding, the US Government was forced to "shut down". It was, as usual, a shutdown more honoured in the breach: Eighty-three per cent of the supposedly defunded government was carrying on as usual, impervious to whatever restraints the people's representatives might wish to impose, and the 800,000 workers deemed "non-essential" had been assured that, when it was all over, they would be paid in full for all the days they had to spend with their feet up at home.

But out in the wilds of America's many areas of natural beauty it was a different story. The "National Park Service" is responsible for canyons and glaciers and the like, which one would not have thought required much attending to during a "shutdown". Nevertheless, the NPS decided to expend far more resources attempting to close open-air, unfenced wilderness than it would normally do in keeping it open. In my book *The [Un]documented Mark Steyn*, I noted one particular vignette from the NPS stormtroopers' crackdown - the story of a group of elderly tourists from Europe, Asia and Australia whose bus was trapped deep in Yellowstone Park on the day the shutdown began:

> *They were pulled over photographing a herd of bison when an armed ranger informed them, with the insouciant ad-hoc unilateral lawmaking to which the armed bureaucrat is distressingly prone, that taking photographs counts as illegal 'recreation'. 'Sir, you are recreating,' the ranger informed the tour guide. And we can't have that, can we?*
>
> *They were ordered back to the Old Faithful Inn, next to the famous geyser of the same name, but forbidden to leave*

said inn to look at said geyser. Armed rangers were posted at the doors, and, just in case one of the wily Japanese or Aussies managed to outwit his captors by escaping through one of the inn's air ducts and down to the scenic attraction, a fleet of NPS SUVs showed up every hour and a half throughout the day, ten minutes before Old Faithful was due to blow, to surround the geyser and additionally ensure that any of America's foreign visitors trying to photograph the impressive natural phenomenon from a second-floor hotel window would still wind up with a picture full of government officials.

The following morning the bus made the two-and-a-half-hour journey to the park boundary but was prevented from using any of the bathrooms en route, including at a private dude ranch whose owner was threatened with the loss of his license if he allowed any tourist to use the facilities.

At the same time as the National Park Service was holding legal foreign visitors under house arrest, it was also allowing illegal immigrants to hold a rally on the supposedly closed National Mall. At this bipartisan amnesty bash, the Democrat House minority leader Nancy Pelosi said she wanted to 'thank the President for enabling us to gather here' and Republican Congressman Mario Diaz-Balart also expressed his gratitude to the administration for 'allowing us to be here'.

Eight centuries after Magna Carta, this is how America's barons - well, "baroness" in the case of Nancy Pelosi - talk about their sovereign. But it's not King Barack's land; it's supposed to be the people's land, and his most groveling and unworthy subjects shouldn't require a dispensation by His Benign Majesty to set foot on it. It is disturbing how easily large numbers of Americans lapse into a neo-monarchical prostration that few subjects of actual monarchies would be comfortable with these days.

But then in actual monarchies the king takes a more generous view of "public lands". Two years after Magna Carta, in 1217, King Henry III signed the Charter of the Forest, which despite various amendments and replacement statutes remained in force in Britain for some three-quarters of a millennium, until the early Seventies. If Magna Carta is a landmark in its concept of individual rights, the Forest Charter played an equivalent role in advancing the concept of the commons, the public space. Repealing various restrictions by his predecessors, Henry III opened the royal forests to the freemen of England, granted extensive grazing and hunting rights, and eliminated the somewhat severe penalty of death for taking the king's venison. The National Park Service have not yet fried anyone for shooting King Barack's deer, but they are willing to put you under house arrest for shooting a holiday snap of it. It is somewhat sobering to reflect that an English peasant enjoyed more freedom on the sovereign's land in the 13th century than a freeborn American does on "the people's land" in the 21st century.

History is not a straight line. There are times when liberty is on the march, and times when it is in retreat. With the exception of sexual license - which these days is about the only thing you don't need a license for - individual liberty is having a very rocky start to the new millennium.

So, in unpromising times, Chris Berg and John Roskam have written an indispensable guide to the significance of this anniversary. As they explain, they have a preference for the definite article - "*the* Magna Carta" rather than "Magna Carta". In the preceding pages, I have eschewed the definite article, in part because things seem a lot more indefinite than they used to. In his poem

"What Say the Reeds at Runnymede?", Kipling was confident enough to write:

And still when mob or Monarch lays
Too rude a hand on English ways,
The whisper wakes, the shudder plays,
Across the reeds at Runnymede...

Is that still true in England? And America, Canada, Australia? Does the whisper still wake, the shudder still play? Across the Anglosphere, the beneficiaries of an 800-year inheritance seem to be losing the habits of liberty - and, once that happens, only darkness lies ahead. Better to re-learn the old lessons while we still can.

PREFACE

The Magna Carta is the product of a revolt against excessive and unjust taxation. In the eight hundred years since King John put his seal on the Magna Carta, dozens of books have been written about the document. Many more works have been published in 2015. Yet, while much scholarship is devoted to exploring the history of the Magna Carta, often its significance and relevance is overlooked.

To a modern reader the Magna Carta's language is obscure and its provisions are anachronistic. But this is only because the mechanisms by which medieval English governments expropriated the property of their citizens are different to those of our own time. The royal government of medieval England was a vast apparatus designed to extract as much money as possible out of the people and their property.

In June 1215 a group of barons forced King John to agree to

the Magna Carta, which contained a list of concessions and limitations on the monarch's power to tax his subjects. While historians still argue about whether the Magna Carta should be regarded as a peace treaty, or a contract, or a proto-constitution, its long term significance as a constraint on the power to tax is undeniable. Long after questions on matters of scutage, amercements, and socage ceased to be relevant, the Magna Carta remained an icon of resistance to unjust taxation. It is still a warning to rulers that the power to tax is not unlimited.

Ultimately the limits to taxation embedded in the Magna Carta took on a life of their own, giving us the essential building blocks of modern democratic liberty. From the provisions of the Magna Carta came the principle of the rule of law—that every person, including the king, is subject to the law. The Magna Carta is also key to the development of the English common law, whose principle that law should evolve gradually and organically is one of the foundations of a liberal legal order. All this came from the Magna Carta's limits on the power of the state to tax.

This book explores how the Magna Carta irrevocably made the relationship between tax and liberty the great liberal cause throughout centuries of English and then British history. We explain what the Magna Carta means for liberty and freedom of the individual.

There are a plethora of books on the Magna Carta for those interested in learning more about the subject. The gold standard in Magna Carta studies is William McKechnie's *Magna Carta: A Commentary on the Great Charter of King John, with an Historical Introduction*. McKechnie was a professor of law at the University of Glasgow. His commentary on the Magna Carta, first published in 1905, with a second edition appearing in 1914, continues to be the single best analysis of the text and meaning of the

Magna Carta. A century on, McKechnie's language and writing remain fresh and engaging.

The second edition of *Magna Carta*, published in 1992 by Sir James Clarke Holt, a professor of medieval history at Cambridge University, is the most important work on the law and politics of the period. David Carpenter's *Magna Carta*, which appeared in 2015, incorporates the latest scholarship on the document's origins and provisions and is indispensable. Other works, all of which are recent and interesting, include *Magna Carta: A Very Short Introduction* and *Magna Carta: The Foundation of Freedom 1215-2015* by Nicholas Vincent, *Magna Carta: The Making and Legacy of the Great Charter* by Dan Jones, *King John: England, Magna Carta and the Making of a Tyrant* by Stephen Church, and *King John: Treachery, Tyranny and the Road to Magna Carta* by Marc Morris.

William Blackstone's *Commentaries on the Laws of England* were the result of a highly successful and highly remunerative series of lectures he delivered in the 1760s. The *Commentaries* were hugely influential in the development of the common law in England and the United States and helped establish the modern-day standing of the Magna Carta. The *Commentaries* are available online and for free through the Online Library of Liberty.

Readers interested in twelfth and thirteenth century politics and society will do no better than turning to two comprehensive overviews: A. L. Poole's 1951 *From Domesday Book to Magna Carta, 1087-1216*, part of the Oxford History of England, and the more recent *England under the Norman and Angevin Kings, 1075-1225* by Robert Bartlett, which is part of the New Oxford History of England series.

Books are collaborative efforts, and this no less than others. This book would not be possible without the incomparable assistance of

PREFACE

Stephanie Forrest, our researcher and editor. Stephanie's detailed, insightful, and scholarly work provides the foundation on which many of this book's arguments rest. We would also like to thank the ever-cheerful and helpful Carla Schodde for her Latin translations. Aline Le Guen, Ben Hourigan, Peter Gregory, Patrick Hannaford, Darcy Allen, and James Bolt also made many thoughtful suggestions on the text.

Finally, a short note on terminology. Magna Carta is Latin for 'Great Charter'. In some scholarly work it is called simply 'Magna Carta'—that is, without the definite article 'the'. Throughout this book 'Magna Carta' is called 'the Magna Carta' for no other reason than to assist in the readability of the work. We have applied the same principle to names, titles, and places. Where a variety of terminologies are available we have chosen the simplest and most understandable.

We have not sought to write a book buried in scholarly exegesis, but something that brings the Magna Carta into the present day—a book that illustrates the enduring significance of the document and the tax revolt from which it emerged.

Chris Berg & John Roskam
May 2015

THE ANGEVIN EMPIRE
UNDER HENRY II

SCOTLAND

Edinburgh

IRELAND

Dublin

WALES

ENGLAND

London
Runnymede

Bouvines

NORMANDY

Paris

BRITTANY

MAINE

LANDS OF THE
KING OF FRANCE

ANJOU

POITOU

AQUITAINE

Bordeaux

GASCONY

TOULOUSE

Lands inherited by Henry II

Lands acquired through Henry's
marriage to Eleanor of Aquitaine

Lands acquired through conquest
and diplomacy

Disputed lands claimed by
Henry II

INTRODUCTION

The Magna Carta made the modern world. Our understanding of liberty, democracy, and human rights are all in some way related to what was inscribed on parchment at Runnymede, a field outside London, in June 1215.

Yet to read the Magna Carta in translation, it is not at all obvious how this document led to the great liberal reforms and revolutions of subsequent centuries. The document, a few thousand words in Latin, outlines how the English King John, who ruled between 1199 and 1216, could tax his subjects.

The Magna Carta enshrined the rule of law—the idea that the king is subject to the law. But establishing the principle that the law applies to the king as well as to everyone else doesn't resolve the question of what 'the law' is, or whether the law is good or bad. What the rule of law establishes is that the power of the king

1

is not unlimited. Today we take it for granted that there are some things a government cannot do to its citizens. Eight hundred years ago such a concept was revolutionary.

The Magna Carta says nothing about 'parliament', and what we recognise today as the first meeting of parliament didn't take place until 1265, half a century after the Magna Carta. Yet during the English Civil War, in the conflict between the king and the parliament, the Magna Carta was cited as the guarantee of the right of parliament to hold the monarch to account. The radical Levellers fighting against the dictatorship of Oliver Cromwell relied on the Magna Carta for their arguments. Richard Overton believed it was the 'brazen wall, and impregnable Bulwalk that defends the Common liberty of England from all illegal & destructive Arbitrary Power whatsoever, be it either Prince or State endeavoured.'

The Magna Carta says nothing about 'freedom of the press'. Indeed such a concept would have been difficult for anyone at Runnymede to comprehend. Yet in the eighteenth century the Magna Carta was utilised by radicals like John Wilkes to argue against government censorship of the press. Arthur Beardmore, a friend of Wilkes, was arrested in 1762 after he published an article attacking the prime minister. Beardmore ensured he was arrested in his home while teaching his son about the Magna Carta. The event was captured in a popular and widely published engraving.

The struggles for suffrage and democracy in the nineteenth and twentieth centuries rested their claims for liberty on the ancient document. The People's Charter of 1838 consciously echoed the Magna Carta. The Chartists regarded their call for universal male suffrage, salaried MPs, the abolition of property qualifications, secret ballots, electorates of equal size, and annual parliaments as a continuation of the process of political reform commenced by the Magna Carta. The suffragettes cited the Magna Carta in support of their argument for votes for women. After her release from imprisonment for breaching the peace in 1908, Christabel Pankhurst declared that 'the British constitution provides that taxation and representation shall go together. Therefore, women taxpayers are entitled to the vote'. To Nelson Mandela, apartheid was incompatible with eight centuries of British history. In 1964, at his trial for sabotage that would result in his 27 year imprisonment, Nelson Mandela said from the dock:

> From my reading of Marxist literature and from conversations with Marxists, I have gained the impression that communists regard the parliamentary system of the West as undemocratic and reactionary. But, on the contrary, I am an admirer of such a system. The Magna Carta, the Petition of Rights, and the Bill of Rights are documents which are held in veneration by democrats throughout the world.
>
> I have great respect for British political institutions, and for the country's system of justice. I regard the British Parliament as the most democratic institution in the world, and the independence and impartiality of its judiciary never fail to arouse my admiration.

In the twenty-first century 'Magna Carta' has become a byword for something which protects individual rights. Tim Berners-Lee, credited with inventing the internet, has called for an 'online Magna Carta' to protect the rights of internet users against government regulation.

All of this started at Runnymede.

CHAPTER
ONE

THE PARCHMENT SEALED AT RUNNYMEDE

Runnymede is today an unimposing place. A forty minute drive from the centre of London, it is a 100-metre-wide strip of meadow by the side of the Thames. A crop of trees separates the meadow from a two-lane road. In the meadow is a small, faux-Greek rotunda on a platform. In the middle of the rotunda is a granite pillar which reads: 'To Commemorate Magna Carta—Symbol of Freedom Under Law'.

The rotunda is not British. It was built by the American Bar Association with voluntary contributions from 9,000 American lawyers at the cost of $30,000. An American newspaper reported that the rotunda was the memorial 'that the British had for 742 years neglected to erect'. Five thousand people attended the opening ceremony on 28 July 1957, a sunny Sunday afternoon.

In the midst of the Cold War, and just a year after the crushing of the Hungarian Revolution by the Soviet Union, the event commemorating the Magna Carta took on a special significance. Charles S. Rhyne, the president-elect of the American Bar Association, declared in his speech:

> The world today is at a crucial point in the struggle between freedom and tyranny. On the one side are those who stand in the tradition of Magna Carta and defend the right of men to be free. On the other side stand the forces of darkness, who would deny freedom and exalt the state. This monument dramatizes the fundamental difference between our system of government, with its recognition of individual rights, and the Communist system, which denies such rights…
>
> There are men today who profess to see no great difference between Communist and anti-Communist regimes. They do not perceive what this monument represents and what Communism stands for. That difference is measured by the phrase: Freedom under law.

As president of the American Bar Association, Rhyne established 1 May as 'Law Day' because May Day was commemorated by communist parties around the world. Five years later, Rhyne won a landmark Supreme Court case—*Baker v. Carr*—which helped established the principle that electoral districts were required to be the same size to ensure 'one person, one vote'.

Another speaker at the opening was the Right Honourable Sir Hartley Shawcross, Q.C., M.P., chairman of the Bar Council of England and Wales. He was a Labour MP and had been the chief prosecutor for the United Kingdom at the Nuremberg war crimes trials. Shawcross eulogised the Magna Carta as a defence against tyranny, and he pointed out, 'Sometimes the activities of even popularly elected legislatures infringe on liberty. The tyranny of the majority is still tyranny.' And he spoke about the dangers of 'the excesses of bureaucracy' and the special place of lawyers in the twentieth century:

> As the modern state becomes more complex and the interventions of government more frequent, considerations of easier administration or more expeditious governmental action are too frequently allowed to override the judicial assessment of private rights.

While there had been no formal monument to commemorate what occurred at Runnymede until American lawyers helpfully stepped in, the Magna Carta has always loomed large in the English mind. George VI's private secretary recorded a revealing moment during the Second World War when he was driving with the king a few weeks after D-Day. George had been frustrated by the growing power of the office of prime minister under Winston Churchill. Suddenly, the king 'threw his arm out of the window and exclaimed "And that's where it all started". We were passing Runnymede.'

Why Runnymede? The field was halfway between the base of the barons, at Staines-upon-Thames, and Windsor Castle, where King John was headquartered. On one side of the meadow was a marsh and on the other was a stream of the Thames, meaning the two sides approached each other head-on. Given the king and the barons were at war, it was important that no side could encircle or surprise the other. Yet Runnymede wasn't just a neutral halfway point. It had its own important history. The name probably comes from the Anglo-Saxon word for regular meeting—'runieg'—and meadow—'mede'. Before the Norman Conquest of

1066, the site was possibly used for meetings of the 'witenagemot', the proto-parliament comprising secular and ecclesiastical nobility convened by Anglo-Saxon kings. Nevertheless, Runnymede was an obscure enough location that the text of the Magna Carta itself contains an explanation of the site, noting that the agreement had been made 'in the meadow which is called Runnymede, between Windsor and Staines'.

There are many things we don't know about what happened at Runnymede. The discussions at Runnymede were the culmination of a sequence of events that began in early 1215 when a number of barons had renounced their oath of loyalty to King John. The king's offer to put the dispute to arbitration had been rejected by the rebels. On 12 May, John effectively declared war on the rebels by ordering the seizure of their castles. Forces opposing John occupied London on Sunday 17 May while many Londoners were at Mass. At the end of the month John offered letters of safe conduct for the barons' negotiators to meet at Runnymede, where the king himself appeared on 10 June.

Precisely where at Runnymede the king and the barons met is not known. It may have been held where the rotunda now stands, or on a small island in the middle of the Thames, no more than two or three acres in size. Or perhaps it was on land over which the Thames now flows. Over eight centuries the river has shifted its course. What tourists see today is different from what existed in 1215.

The king and the barons had a series of meetings over the course of more than a week. From the documentary evidence, we know John and at least the 27 bishops and barons listed in the Magna Carta were in attendance, but it is unknown who else was there. The language spoken at Runnymede was French. There are many surviving eyewitness accounts of events from the period that were regarded as important and significant. For example, we know in great detail what occurred at the coronation of Richard I in September 1189. The fact that there are no eyewitness accounts of the days at Runnymede reveals, perhaps, that those there did not attach the same significance to what occurred as later generations have. If there were any depictions of the events of June 1215 they haven't survived. Presumably, meetings took place in tents but they could just as easily have been out in the open. Also unknown is the process of negotiation. A document called the 'Articles of the Barons' has survived and is now in the British Library. This document seems to be an early draft of an agreement between John and the barons. Nearly all of the provisions in the Articles of the Barons appear in the Magna Carta. The Articles were perhaps themselves a product of earlier versions of the barons' demands. The 'Unknown Charter of Liberties' (so-called because it only became known in 1893), likely to have originated some months before Runnymede, incorporated some of what was in the Articles and then what was in the Magna Carta itself.

It might be a surprise to those discovering the Magna Carta for the first time that the date of the Magna Carta is debated. The 15th of June is traditionally celebrated as its anniversary, and 'Given by our hand in the meadow that is called Runnymede between Windsor and Staines, on the fifteenth day of June in the seventeenth year of our reign' is what is written in the final line of the document. But this doesn't necessarily mean this was the date of final agreement. The date may have been included in the Magna Carta prior to the final agreement over its terms. James Holt, one of the foremost historians of the Magna Carta, has argued that 19 June was the date on which it could be said the Magna Carta was finalised, because that was the day on which the barons swore an oath of loyalty to John and in return he agreed to stop acts of war against the barons.

What occurred between 10 June and 19 June can only ever be the subject of informed speculation—but the weight of evidence is that the terms of the Magna Carta were agreed on 15 June and that is thus the appropriate date to commemorate it.

Confusion as to the official date of historic documents is not uncommon. In 1776, 56 delegates to the Second Continental Congress in Philadelphia signed the Declaration of Independence. While this anniversary is celebrated on 4 July, some historians argue it was signed in August.

Nor was the Magna Carta *signed* at Runnymede. It's not known whether King John could write. No known example of his handwriting exists. The Magna Carta was 'sealed' by the attachment of the king's wax seal, which certified it was an official royal document. The person who attached the seal was an official in the royal chancery called the 'spigurnel'.

It is likewise not known whether there ever was a single 'master copy' of the Magna Carta. Instead, what we have today are four copies of the Magna Carta, each of which historians are reasonably certain were created at Runnymede, and each of which have an equal status as 'the Magna Carta'. Each is termed an 'engrossment'. Of the four surviving engrossments of the Magna Carta, two are displayed in the British Library, one is in Lincoln Cathedral, and one in Salisbury Cathedral.

It is estimated that to write out a single copy of the Magna Carta would have taken about eight hours. From the analysis of the script of each of the four engrossments, it is assumed that each was written by a different person. The ink used by the scribes was made from the sap of oak trees mixed with soot. The scribes wrote the Magna Carta on parchment, which is treated sheep's skin. Parchment is not absorbent in the way that paper is, and as the words were etched into the parchment, the ink's interaction with the parchment began a chemical reaction which explains why the words still remain clearly legible.

How many engrossments of the Magna Carta were made at Runnymede is a mystery. The purpose of making multiple engrossments was to have them distributed throughout the country. Some historians speculate perhaps up to fifty engrossments were made, while others suggest that if they were sent only to bishop's dioceses no more than thirteen engrossments were produced.

The Magna Carta was amended and then reissued in the years following 1215, first by John's son, Henry III, and then by Henry's son, Edward I. So there is a 'Magna Carta' of 1216, 1217, 1225, 1297, and 1300. In addition to the four engrossments surviving from 1215, there is one from 1216, four from 1217, four from 1225, four from 1297, and five or six (the authenticity of one is questioned) extant from 1300. In addition the Magna Carta was also reissued in 1265, although no original copies of a 1265 edition survive. That is why it is possible to talk of the '1225 Magna Carta', which for many years was far better known than that of 1215, or the '1297 Magna Carta', of which one of the four existing copies is owned by the Australian Parliament.

The Magna Carta was written in medieval Latin. Its English translation is approximately 3,500 words. On the original parchment, it is a continuous text without headings or paragraph breaks. The different sections of the document were identified by prominent capital letters. It was the great legal historian William Blackstone who in 1759 divided the Magna Carta into separate chapters that broadly matched the different sections of the document. Blackstone gave the 1215 Magna Carta its 63 chapters, and his system of chapter numbering has remained in use to this day.

There are numerous translations into English of the Magna

Carta and all have slight differences. Translations must accommodate the fact that the meanings of words change over time, and every language has its own ambiguities and subtleties. Two historians might translate the same word in quite different ways. Even in English the same word can have quite different connotations to different people. Terms such as 'rights', 'liberties', 'free man', and 'realm' are all in the Magna Carta, and two people reading it might have two similar, yet differing, interpretations of what exactly is a 'right'. Matters become even more complicated when it is appreciated that words in the Magna Carta, such as 'free man', have meanings that vary according to their context and the chapters in which they appear.

For instance, the most famous chapter of the Magna Carta is Chapter 39. Over the centuries it came to be interpreted as guaranteeing to every citizen a trial by jury, and according to the due process of the law. Yet as significant as this chapter is there is no agreed English translation of it. This is the original Latin text from one of the four 'original' copies of the Magna Carta:

> *Nullus liber homo capiatur, vel inprisonetur, aut dissaisiatur, aut utlaghetur, aut exuletur, aut aliquo modo destruatur, nec super eum ibimus, nec super eum mittemus, nisi per legale iuditium parium suorum vel per legem terre.*

Here is the translation of Chapter 39 by one modern eminent historian of the Magna Carta:

> No free man will be taken or imprisoned or disseised or outlawed or exiled or in any way ruined, nor shall we go or send against him, save by the lawful judgement of his peers and by the law of the land.

This is another translation by an equally eminent modern historian:

No free man is to be arrested, or imprisoned, or disseised, or outlawed, or exiled, or in any way destroyed, nor will we go against him, nor will we send against him, save by the lawful judgement of his peers or by the law of the land.

There are some minor differences between these two translations. 'Taken' has a different meaning from 'arrested', as does 'ruined' from 'destroyed'. A major difference is how the word *vel* is translated. In Latin *vel* normally means 'or' but in some circumstances it can mean 'and'. Punishment according to a free man's peers *and* the law of the land is quite different from punishment according to either one's peers *or* the law of the land. Under the former interpretation, the law of the land must still be followed regardless of the judgement of the peers of the accused. Under the latter, the judgement of the accused's peers is sufficient. Given that in many cases the peers of the accused know the accused and would be susceptible to their influence, either for their advantage or against it, whether *vel* means 'or' or 'and' makes a difference. Profound differences in political philosophy might pivot on this translation. If the correct word is 'and', this suggests that the judgment of one's peers is constrained by law. If the correct word is 'or', then this suggests the judgement of one's peers is an alternative to the law. In the former, the law is sovereign. In the latter, the will of the community is sovereign.

The Magna Carta is full of such ambiguities. Chapter 40, nearly as renowned as Chapter 39, demonstrates that even a short sentence can give rise to confusion. Some translations have Chapter 40 as 'To no one shall we sell, to no one shall we deny or delay right or justice', while others have it as 'To no one will we sell, to no one will we deny or delay, right or justice'. In English the difference between 'shall' and 'will' is one of both tone and intention. Both translations are equally valid but each have slightly different meanings.

Then there is the question of what the Magna Carta actually *is*. Is it a piece of legislation, or a contract between the king and the barons, or a peace treaty between them, or something else? The determination of these legal niceties have never been settled and at various times arguments have been presented for all of these alternatives.

In medieval England a 'charter' was a grant from the king of rights, usually over land. In the Magna Carta, the document itself is described as a *carta* (charter). In the immediate aftermath of June 1215, what was agreed at Runnymede was described as 'the charter of liberties which the lord king has granted in common to the barons of England'. In 1217, those ruling in the name of the boy king Henry III reissued the Magna Carta, as had occurred the previous year, and at the same time issued another charter that regulated the royal forests. The Magna Carta was the longer of the two charters, and so to distinguish it from the Forest Charter it was described as the *maiori carta*, meaning the longer or greater charter.

Whatever the Magna Carta might now symbolise, the barons themselves did not regard the document as a statement of rights granted by the king. They considered it to be a statement of rights that had *always* existed. King John was merely confirming he would uphold those rights. In a technical sense, the Magna Carta formally became part of the laws of England when a parliament convened by Edward I in 1297 confirmed the provisions of the 1225 Magna Carta.

Over the centuries, various chapters of the Magna Carta have been repealed. Today only four of its chapters remain on the statute books: Chapter 1, which guarantees the Church freedom from interference from the monarch; Chapter 13, which gives London special privileges as a city; and Chapters 39 and 40, which deal with the right to a fair trial.

The Magna Carta is a document very much of its time. It reflects the social, political and economic structures of the thirteenth century: the economic and political hierarchy of feudalism. Thus the document opens with King John's titles:

Johannes dei gratia Rex Anglie, Dominus Hibernie, Dux Normannie et Aquitannie, Comes Andegavie

John, by the grace of God, king of England, lord of Ireland, duke of Normandy and Aquitaine, count of Anjou

This description was part fact, part politics, part fantasy. John was unambiguously the king of England, albeit a king whose grip on power looked tenuous in June 1215. He termed himself 'lord' of Ireland instead of 'king', because given the complicated politics of Ireland, he regarded himself as ruling it in a personal capacity. He did hold parts of Aquitaine in France but had lost Normandy and Anjou a decade previously. By 1215, his titles of Duke of Normandy and Count of Anjou were purely ceremonial—a sad memory of the patrimony that had been lost.

Where the Magna Carta refers to 'barons', and 'earls', and 'knights', the situation becomes more complicated. The barons are the group most associated with the Magna Carta. The Latin for barons, *barones*, is used throughout the document. To understand the significance of the barons, a brief explanation of English society in 1215 is necessary.

In theory and in law, all the land in medieval England was owned by the king. All of those below the king had rights only to use land. They did not have ownership in the way the concept is understood today. In exchange for the right to use the land, landholders provided services to the king, originally in the form of personal military service and the provision of knights. Over time, military service was increasingly commuted into money payments.

Those who held land directly from the king, his 'tenants-in-chief', in turn allowed the land they held to be possessed and used by 'tenants' and 'sub-tenants' also in return for services. These hierarchies formed the basis of the feudal system.

The word 'feudal' comes from the Latin *feudum* meaning 'fief'—a fief being property held by a tenant in return for service. 'Vassal' is the term applied to an individual who held land from the king or an overlord, under an obligation to provide services or money for their holdings.

The idea that the land was the king's, and that his vassals occupied his land under sufferance, had far-reaching consequences. It gave the king the power to control who his vassals married, because upon marriage the wife's land came to be controlled by her husband. Kings would seek to prevent land falling into the possession of their opponents through marriage. This was the context of Chapter 8, which says that widows holding land through the king could not marry without royal consent. To gain the king's consent, a payment had to be made to the crown.

Nevertheless, the absence of a strictly-defined, separate aristocracy is one of the features that was to distinguish England from continental Europe in future centuries. One of the foremost historians of the thirteenth century has noted that:

> [what] emerges from both official documentation and literary sources is that there was technically no noble class in England during this period. Although there were earls, barons, and knights—all of whom it is certainly sensible to regard as aristocrats—there was no unified group of nobles with privileges that marked them off from the rest of the population.

The Domesday Book, completed in 1086, gives a glimpse of the distribution of land holdings in medieval England. Excluding towns and four northern shires that weren't surveyed, the annual income of the land assessed in the Domesday Book in the currency of the period was about £73,000. The church received around 26 per cent of that income, and the king and his family received around 24 per cent. The king's officials received around 2 per cent, and another 5 per cent went to trusted associates of the king. The rest of the income of the country—more than 40 per cent—went to the approximately 170 barons who had helped William conquer England after 1066. A century and a half later the situation was not much different. Henry III said there were 200 men in England who mattered and he knew them all.

'Baron' was not a title or an honorific as was 'Earl' or 'Duke'. Barons can best be thought of as magnates—large landholders. In the context of the Magna Carta, a baron was someone in a particular legal relationship with the crown. Barons usually held land directly from the king. A baron could be a layperson or a member of a religious order. The wealth of the barons varied greatly and depended on a number of factors, including the size of their holdings. An assessment under Henry II of the service due to him from earls and barons showed that some owed him service of twenty knights, while others owed him service of 100 knights. It has been estimated that of the approximately 200 barons in England in 1215, 40 were in rebellion against John, 40 were supporters of John, and the remaining 120 were undeclared.

The second chapter of the Magna Carta specifies that when an earl or baron died, their heir would have to pay no more than £100 to inherit their estate. Effectively the payment (called a 'relief') is what today would be termed a death duty or an inheritance tax. The fact that the first chapter of the Magna Carta was about the rights of the Church and the second chapter was about how much heirs were required to pay to inherit a barony reveals just how important the barons regarded the matter. Chapter 3 of the Magna Carta specifies that if an heir was underage when the earl or baron died, they could have their inheritance when they came of age without the payment. The justification for this provision was that heirs who were not yet 21 years old were wards of the crown, and the crown enjoyed the benefits of the heir's estates until the heir attained adulthood. Why this was so goes to the essence of feudalism. Land was held in return for military service, and because a child could not bear arms the land reverted to the crown until that service could be performed. At any one time, the king might control up to a dozen wards. As they were underage, the king had the right to control who they were to marry.

Chapter 3 of the Magna Carta also mentions earls and knights. Earls had specific titles, and earldoms were created by the king. Under William the Conqueror there were seven earldoms in England. The title of the earl was taken from the county where they had the right to collect a third of the profits of the county court. Historians put the number of earls during John's reign at twelve.

The position of knight (*milites* in the Magna Carta) is perhaps the most confusing to modern readers. A knight could be someone who was 'knighted', or who had a specified military role, or simply someone who was recognised as a knight in their community. Knights could hold land from the king, from barons, or the church. The task of defining who were knights is difficult, but taking into account all of these factors, it has been estimated there were 4,500 men acknowledged as knights at the time of the Magna Carta. Chapter 2 specifies that heirs of knights were required to pay at most 100 shillings for their inheritance. As there were 20 shillings to the pound, the price of a knight's inheritance was no more than one-twentieth that of a baron's.

To think of knights during King John's reign as the landed gentry would be an anachronism, but at the same time there are parallels that help us understand the central role knights played in the administration of justice and local government during the period. Chapter 18 of the Magna Carta specified that four times a year in each county, four knights from that county and two judges would hear lawsuits about disputed property. Similarly, Chapter 48 demonstrates how central knights were to the administration of government. In this chapter, John promised the barons in each county that there would be an investigation of the forest laws by twelve knights chosen by the 'worthy men of the county'. The chapter was one of the first implemented following the meeting at Runnymede.

The 'royal forest' was land controlled directly by the king over which he had exclusive and largely personal jurisdiction. Some of the 'forest' might be forest as we understand it today, but it also included cultivated land and villages. Under John, around one-third of England was classified as part of the royal forest. Special laws applied to the royal forest and to the land adjacent to the forest. These included limits on the hunting of wild animals, the grazing of farm animals, and the collecting of wood. Those who broke forest laws were subject to brutal punishments (the penalty of killing deer in the royal forest was blinding and castration) or exorbitant fines.

Royal forests were more than hunting grounds for the king. They had an important financial role. Up to half of the crown's revenue could come from the royal forest. Under Henry II, large areas of England were 'afforested'—brought into the domain of the royal forest—and this was one of the major reasons for popular discontent during Henry's reign. To generate revenue the sons of Henry II, Richard and John, disafforested land in exchange for financial payments.

Indeed, the story of the Magna Carta is about the voracious taxation and revenue collection of Henry's sons.

CHAPTER
TWO

THE POWER TO TAX

T ax is central to the history of personal liberty. The three touchstone events in the development of human rights and freedoms—the Magna Carta, the English Civil War, and the American Revolution—all have their foundation in a fight against what was regarded as unjust taxation by the government. The rebellion against John by the barons was a tax revolt. The Magna Carta is a document about taxation. No less than 45 of its 63 chapters deal with the collection of taxes and payments to the king. To understand why the Magna Carta is so significant, we need to understand it as the result of a rebellion against a monarch who tried to overtax his subjects.

'The power to "tax" is simply the power to "take"', the Nobel laureate James M. Buchanan and Geoffrey Brennan have written. Tax is the primary and most powerful way the state imposes itself on the people it rules. Governments exist through the coercive appropriation of resources from others. This is true whether those resources are used for good or bad—whether it is used to purchase so-called 'public goods' for the benefit of the citizenry, or whether it is simply used to enrich the ruling elite. The development of constitutional government has been the long and fraught process to build a system whereby the subjects of taxation can give their consent to that taxation. Nevertheless, in democratic and non-democratic systems alike the ability of governments to unilaterally extract labour, goods, or money from their population has always been a source of resentment. Regardless of the ideology that underpins the state, the state has a monopoly of force which it can use to coerce its subjects to pay more tax than its subjects consider just.

Redistributing resources by force is the fundamental business of government. The desire of states for more finances is infinite. Rulers, whether democratic or dictatorial, use the mechanisms of government to distribute rewards to their supporters. The key to staying in power for any ruler is to minimise the exertions they place on their supporters and maximise the benefits of support. The necessary size of those benefits will be determined by the likelihood of supporters swapping their allegiance to challengers.

Corvée labour developed as the imposition of tax (paid through labour) on a class of subjects who were unlikely to challenge the ruler yet were not wealthy enough to provide the ruler with the material support they sought. Another technique for minimising the tax burden on a ruler's supporters is to expropriate wealth from those outside the political community. By invading other territories, rulers can loot freely without any risk to their supporters at home.

The earliest states—tribal chiefdoms—extracted resources from those under their jurisdiction through payments that resembled a combination of rent, tribute, and taxation. Taxes could be levied on goods—for instance, a certain amount of wheat paid in tribute to a ruler—or on labour. In the Bible, Samuel warned the Israelites about the behaviour of kings:

> This is what the king who will reign over you will claim as his rights: He will take your sons and make them serve with his chariots and horses, and they will run in front of his chariots. Some he will assign to be commanders of thousands and commanders of fifties, and others to plow his ground and reap his harvest, and still others to make weapons of war and equipment for his chariots. He will take your daughters to be perfumers and cooks and bakers. He will take the best of your fields and vineyards and olive groves and give them to his attendants. He will take a tenth of your grain and of your vintage and give it to his officials and attendants. Your male and female servants and the best of your cattle and donkeys he will take for his own use. He will take a tenth of your flocks, and you yourselves will become his slaves.

Samuel was right, of course, and the Israelite kings made extensive use of forced labour for building and agricultural labour.

Tax revolts are a political and social phenomenon common across many epochs, cultures, and regions on the planet. It is striking how central the question of taxation has been to the institutional development of the free society. A Sumerian proverb reads: 'You can have a Lord, you can have a King, but the man to fear is the tax collector.' The earliest record we have of political change driven by tax resistance comes from the Ancient Sumerian city-state of Lagesh around 2350 BC.

Lagesh, now in south-western Iraq, was ruled by Lugalanda, an oppressive and harsh ruler who imposed 'high and multifarious taxes' on his people. Farmers who brought their sheep to the city temple for shearing were charged for the privilege. Officials came to funerals to confiscate offerings. Divorce was taxed. Lagesh's constant warfare was funded from the expropriation of land, cattle, and other resources.

Eventually, the people of Lagesh rose up against these harsh depredations, and installed as king a certain Urukagina, who came from outside the ruling dynasty. Urukagina established one of the world's first legal codes, and he reduced the heavy taxes of his predecessors—such as removing fees for divorce. The reason for his takeover of power is clear—he had a mandate to relieve the oppressive taxation practices of his predecessor. Before Urukagina, 'there were tax collectors' everywhere in Lagesh. After Urukagina, 'there were no tax collectors.'

An outcome of tax resistance is the creation of black markets, or the 'underground economy'—economic activity outside the eye of the state. One particularly heavily taxed ancient economy was Egypt. Tax in Egypt during the third to first centuries BC, like in many premodern states, was collected by tax farmers: individuals contracted to collect taxes on behalf of the state, and who could take a personal profit from what was collected after a specified amount was paid to the government. Until the development of a tax bureaucracy operated by the central government in the eighteenth and nineteenth centuries, 'tax farming' was the usual way taxes were collected.

Chapter 25 of the Magna Carta deals directly with the evils of tax farming under King John—'All shires, hundreds, wapentakes and ridings will be at the ancient farms, without any increment, except our demesne manors.'

Since before the Norman invasion England had been divided into shires. Under the Normans the term 'county' replaced shire as the designation for a large regional area. Counties were divided into sub-districts called 'hundreds' in the south, and in the north 'wapentakes', and 'ridings' in some counties like Yorkshire and Lincolnshire. The king's representative in each county was the sheriff (from the Anglo-Saxon *scir-gerefa* meaning 'shire-reeve', a 'reeve' being an official of the king). The sheriff fulfilled many roles—as the king's tax-gatherer, the local judge, and as the commander of the king's soldiers in the county. The sheriff paid the king for the right to collect taxes in the county—the two key sources of revenue being rent from land owned by the king, and fees and fines from the justice. The position of sheriff was often sold to the highest bidder. The sheriff promised to pay the king an exact amount (a 'farm') and anything received above that (the 'increment') could be kept by the sheriff for himself. The Magna Carta attempted to put an end to the ever-growing increments taken by the sheriff.

Resistance to state taxation is far more common than popular history books have recognised. As the purpose is to *avoid* state power rather than directly *confront* it, we rarely find the sort of records about tax evasion that would help show its extent. We can only see evasion's shadow in the complaints of rulers that their taxes raised far less than would be expected.

Indeed, ancient history is littered with instances of resistance to tax, from colonies revolting against the depredations of distant imperial rulers, to coups and revolutions plotted by the overtaxed rivals of the ruler. David M. Burg's *World History of Tax Rebellions* records an impressive series of ancient tax revolts in the late Roman Republic and early Empire. In 31 BC riots broke out in Rome and across Italy in response to a tax imposed by the emperor Octavian on property owning freedmen. Egyptians rebelled a few years later in response to the heavy demands of Roman tax collectors. In north Africa, a rebellion in response to heavy taxes lasted seven years, between AD 17 to 24. There were further revolts in Gaul in AD 21 and in lower Germany seven years later. In AD 36 an Anatolian tribe tried to flee to the mountains to escape Roman taxation. Three years later a public revolt in Rome itself was put down by Caligula. The Romans objected to Caligula's taxation of everything from luxury goods to prostitution. The revolt in Judea lasting from AD 66 to 70, which ended with the destruction of the Second Temple and the siege of Masada, began with anti-tax protests.

King John is not the only name in English history to be known because of a tax revolt. There are two other famous names—both of women—that history also remembers for resisting oppressive taxation. Boudicca's revolt against the Romans in AD 61 had its origins in tax. Likewise, the legend of Lady Godiva was an anti-tax protest.

Boudicca was the wife of Prasutagus, King of the Iceni, a Celtic tribe that lived in what is now Norfolk and Suffolk. Prasutagus ruled as a nominally independent king allied to the Romans. He was wealthy and took advantage of generous Roman loans. On his death he left his kingdom in the joint custody of his wife and daughters and the Roman emperor. Yet, ignoring his will, the Romans annexed the kingdom. The local Roman procurator, Catus Decianus, having been sent to Britain to extract as much money as possible from the province, looted the lands of Prasutagus. Tacitus records that the dominions of Prasutagus 'were ravaged by the centurions; the slaves pillaged his house, and his effects were seized as lawful plunder … The whole country was considered as a legacy bequeathed to the plunderers'.

The Iceni rebelled under the command of Boudicca. Boudicca brought other tribes into the rebellion. Catus' exactions were not merely targeted at the Iceni. The introduction of a tax on cattle—the *scriptura*—was also much resented. Most of the property of the Britons was in livestock. Local inhabitants were forced to either give up some of their cattle to pay the *scriptura*, or to borrow from Roman moneylenders. These exactions left Roman Britain ripe for rebellion, which the enraged Boudicca was able to exploit. Writing a century after the events he describes, Cassius Dio has Boudicca giving a speech to the assembled rebellious tribes about Roman taxes:

> Have we not been robbed entirely of most of our possessions, and those the greatest, while for those that remain we pay taxes? Besides pasturing and tilling for them all our other possessions, do we not pay a yearly tribute for our very bodies? How much better it would be to have been sold to masters once for all than, possessing empty titles of freedom, to have to ransom ourselves every year! How much better to have been slain and to have perished than to go about with a tax on our heads!

Boudicca besieged and destroyed the Roman city of Colchester, which housed the largest Roman temple in Britain. The temple was maintained by Roman taxes and was a powerful symbol of Roman oppression. Catus Decianus fled to the continent. London, then a fifteen-year-old settlement, was also destroyed by Boudicca. In either AD 60 or 61, in a battle somewhere in the Midlands on a Roman road that came to be known as 'Watling Street', Boudicca was finally defeated. According to Tacitus, 80,000 of her army were killed and Boudicca took poison. The result of the battle was that Roman settlement of the south of England was continued and consolidated.

Likewise, the story of Lady Godiva pivots on resistance to unjust taxation. It was a legend that preoccupied nineteenth century writers. It predated the Norman Conquest and was a story of self-sacrifice that had hints of impropriety. And it was a tale of a woman standing up to her husband in the interests of the people.

The Lady Godiva of the story was based on a real person, 'Godgifu', who lived in the middle of the eleventh century. The tale is told in striking and vivid form by the thirteenth century chronicler Roger of Wendover, a monk at St Albans Abbey. Godgifu was a noblewoman married to Leofric, the Earl of Mercia in the English Midlands and one of the most powerful noblemen on the eve of the Norman Conquest.

According to Roger of Wendover, Leofric had levied heavy taxes on the town of Coventry. The good lady Godiva pleaded with her husband to relieve the town from its heavy burdens. She so exasperated Leofric that he forbade her from speaking on the subject ever again. Godiva continued her entreaties and eventually Leofric offered her a humiliating bargain—if she would ride naked through Coventry he would grant her request:

> Whereupon the countess, beloved of God, loosed her hair and let down her tresses, which covered the whole of her body like a veil, and then mounting her horse and attended by two knights, she rode through the marketplace, without being seen, except her fair legs; and having completed the journey, she returned with gladness to her astonished husband, and obtained of him what she had asked.

Leofric cut Coventry's taxes and issued a charter which confirmed the town's new-found liberties.

Writers retelling the legend from the sixteenth century onwards added more details, including the famous Peeping Tom, who spies on Godiva and is blinded. In that later version of the tale, Godiva ordered all townspeople to stay indoors and shutter their blinds; Tom drilled a hole through his blinds in defiance. Obviously there is symbolism in Godiva's nudity and the way in which she covers herself. The Peeping Tom story also tells us about ideas of privacy and respect.

But in the end, Godiva's story is a story about tax: 'The legend of Lady Godiva's ride remains one of the West's best-known tales of protest against burdensome taxation.' There's no reason to believe that the Godiva story was founded in actual events. For one thing, it was Godiva who ruled Coventry, not Leofric. If she had wanted to relieve the people of Coventry from their burdens, she could have done so herself. To understand how thirteenth century readers understood Lady Godiva's actions, we should focus on why she undertook the journey in the first place, and not on what she was wearing. Roger of Wendover says Godiva relieved Coventry of 'the oppression of a heavy toll'. Roger was a contemporary of King John and his work is one of our main sources for the history of the Magna Carta.

The modern concept of tax—the collection of money by government to spend on general purposes for the ostensible benefit of the whole community—is quite different from tax as understood in the thirteenth century. The medieval state was to a large extent the product of war. War requires money, and that money is collected through taxes. This was true in the time of the Magna Carta and was ultimately the impetus behind the creation of what has been called the English 'tax-based parliamentary state'.

From the time of the Norman Conquest up to the reign of King John, the expectation of both the monarch and his nobles was that the king would finance his expenses from the revenue of his own property. In practice this seldom occurred, mainly because wars were expensive. By the 1130s the king's revenue came primarily from four sources: income from land directly held by the king (40 per cent), payments to the king as a feudal lord (16 per cent), taxation (14 per cent), and payments from the administration of the legal system (12 per cent). These proportions varied year-to-year but they give an indication of the relative importance of each category.

Taxation consisted of levies imposed on the whole population, either in the form of taxes on land or taxes on movables and income. Payments received by the king as feudal lord and from the legal system could be characterised in the language of today as 'fees, fines, and levies'. There were three main kinds of payments John was entitled to collect as a feudal lord—an 'aid', a 'relief', and 'scutage'. In theory, an 'aid' was a voluntary payment from a vassal to their lord to assist the lord with meeting a specific need. Over time it became an expectation that aids would be paid in certain circumstances, such as the payment of a ransom for the lord, the knighting of his eldest son, and funding of the dowry for the first marriage of his eldest daughter. A 'relief' was a payment from a vassal to their lord in order to come into the possession of land.

'Scutage' was a money payment from a vassal to a lord in lieu of providing military service. Traditionally the king expected his direct vassals to provide him with a specified number of knights for forty days a year. During the reign of Henry II, it became clear that the English knights had little interest in fighting on the continent for the king's French territories. Knights' service was grudgingly tendered and the forty day limit meant that the king was constantly negotiating to replenish his forces. The solution was to introduce a payment that could be made as a substitute for service. With these funds the king could hire mercenaries instead. In later decades scutage simply became a tax, with no expectation that it would be paid through military service.

Another form of taxation was the 'tallage'—which was a tax the king could levy at his discretion on land or other forms of property he directly controlled. A particular target of the king's tallage was England's Jewish population. In legal terms, Jews living in medieval England were aliens and the only rights they had were those granted as a courtesy to them by the monarch. There were likely some Jewish inhabitants of England before the Conquest, but the first major Jewish migration to England followed 1066, with a group of Jews from the northern French city of Rouen settling in London. It seems they were invited to England to help finance the new Norman rule. Jews were disproportionally represented in moneylending—it was an attractive industry for the oppressed Jewish peoples across Europe, who were legally barred from owning land. Jews were also able to avoid the Church's ban on usury, as for the most part canon law did not apply to Jews. By the time of the Magna Carta, there were probably no more than five thousand Jews in England. They suffered regular persecution—including, most infamously, a pogrom in March 1190 when York's entire Jewish population of 150 was massacred.

The crown made its protection of the Jews into a mechanism for systematically extracting finance from this segment of society—a segment that, because Christians had been largely pushed out of large scale finance, was gaining a disproportionate share of wealth. From the 1190s an Exchequer of the Jewry was created in order to exploit this financial base, by both enforcing debts and taxing credit. And of course the Jews could provide loans to the king himself. Thus the king's Jews were a source of revenue and credit. It was, furthermore, easier to levy tallage on Jewish moneylenders than the rest of the population. First, their safety was reliant on the king's graces. Second, their wealth was kept as money, rather than goods or land, and so could easily be accounted for.

Many of the tax revolutions of the past were prompted by rates of tax that would now be considered quite low. Today, annual payments of 50 per cent or more of an individual's income are not uncommon. Modern bureaucracies are able to tax much more efficiently, and comprehensively, than their predecessors. Yet it is not the quantum of taxation that counts. As Jean-Baptiste Colbert, the finance minister for King Louis XIV for twenty years, famously said, 'The art of taxation consists in so plucking the goose as to obtain the largest possible amount of feathers with the smallest possible amount of hissing.'

In 1207 King John levied a special one-off tax called the 'Thirteenth'. The rate was set at one shilling to every mark, and because one mark was worth slightly more than thirteen shillings it was called the Thirteenth. It was the equivalent to a 7.5 per cent tax on the value of the property and the annual income of all asset-holders, including the clergy. It was imposed in the face of great unrest and raised the enormous sum of £60,000—at a time when the average yearly income of the king was around £35,000.

> The measures put in place to raise the tax were elaborate and unremitting. Assessment was made by specially appointed justices, who visited every town and parish within their particular county. Fourteen men, for example, were charged with the task in Lincolnshire. In each district, every local man had to appear before them and swear to the value of his rents and moveable goods; the justices made a record of the amount of tax due, which was then passed on to the sheriff for collection. Penalties for evasion were harsh: those found guilty of making false declarations, or otherwise concealing their wealth, were to be cast into prison and have all their goods confiscated for the king's use.

It is no coincidence then that the development of a state bureaucratic apparatus, and intrusion into the private affairs of the
citizenry, develops hand-in-hand with the expansion of a tax system. In order to tax, the government must first account. The first
significant administrative product of the Norman Conquest was
the Domesday Book, ordered by William to determine how much
tax could be collected from his newly acquired kingdom. (The
derivation of the word 'doom' does not refer to future ruin, but to
a final judgement.)

The tax system of medieval England looks impossibly complicated from the vantage point of the twenty-first century. Terms
like the tallage, scutage, and reliefs are alienating and distant. It
could be argued that to apply the word 'tax' to what the medieval state collected from its subjects is inaccurate and that 'extor-
tion' would be a better description. What distinguishes the fiscal
system of King John from our own was its arbitrary nature and
its inefficiency.

In 1776, in his *The Wealth of Nations*, Adam Smith set out four
principles of taxation to which tax systems today still strive to
adhere: equality, certainty, convenience of payment, and economy
of collection. The burden of taxation should be equal on all members of society proportional to their ability to pay. The quantity,
manner, and frequency of payment ought to be certain, allowing
taxpayers to plan around their obligations. Taxes should be levied in a manner and at a time that makes it most convenient to
pay. Finally, governments should keep the costs of collection as
low as possible. The tax system of King John certainly did not
satisfy these principles. Tax was levied at the discretion of the
monarch, was punitive, and was imposed at random times. These
features of the tax system and the oppression it caused gave us
the Magna Carta.

CHAPTER
THREE

ENGLAND BEFORE 1215

Invasions, threatened invasions, civil wars, and threatened civil wars have punctuated two thousand years of British history. One observer writes that 'It is one of the many myths entertained by the English about their history that the country has been free of invasion since the Conquest. In fact there have been at least nine, six of which succeeded.' Those six successful invaders were William the Conqueror in 1066, Stephen in 1135 after the death of Henry I, Queen Isabella who over-threw her husband Edward II in 1327, Henry VI when he was restored to the throne in 1470 during the War of the Roses, Henry Tudor who defeated Richard III and became Henry VII in 1485, and William of Orange in the Glorious Revolution of 1688. The

British Isles have constantly been raided and attacked, and often invaded. On one count there have been more than 70 such instances since 1066.

In the Middle Ages royal succession was an uncertain thing. After the death of Edward the Confessor in 1066, 'the English crown had been seized by force on four occasions by princes who were in blood and worldly outlook essentially French noblemen'— William, Henry I, Stephen, and Henry II.

In the 150 years between the Norman Conquest and King John's war against the barons, England had already seen more than three major civil wars. In 1088, on becoming king, the son of William the Conqueror, William II (known as William Rufus because of his red hair), faced a rebellion from his brother Robert. Between 1135 and 1154 King Stephen fought his cousin Matilda for the throne. And in 1173 Henry II had to fight a civil war against his wife, Eleanor of Aquitaine, and three of his sons, Henry, Richard, and Geoffrey.

In that regard the reign of King John is not very different from the reigns of his predecessors and successors. He precipitated a civil war and at his death he was fighting against a foreign invasion, as had happened many times before and has happened many times since.

One of the most important features of Anglo-Saxon government was the Witenagemot. The Witenagemot was a council of around one hundred nobles and clerics who advised the king. Its origins went back to at least the start of the seventh century. It was not a representative body but it did establish a process whereby a council consulted with and gave advice to the king. At the death of a king, it was the Witenagemot's role to choose the royal successor. When Edward the Confessor died, the nobles and clerics elected Harold, Edward's brother-in-law. Across the channel, William II, Duke of Normandy, argued he had a claim to the throne on the basis of a promise given by Edward. In September 1066, William landed with an army at Pevensey Bay, on the southern English coast. Harold and William met at Hastings in October that year. William won the battle and the throne of England.

William's success at Hastings sparked a wholesale revolution in political, economic, and bureaucratic power in England. The pre-Norman aristocratic elite was almost entirely dispossessed and replaced. A number of Anglo-Saxon nobles fled as far afield as the Byzantine Empire.

The Norman invasion was a hostile invasion. Two decades of violent recriminations, revolts, massacres, and deliberate policies which induced mass starvation followed—particularly in the north. Around 8,000 Normans arrived in England after the invasion, taking control of a country of approximately two million people. Of that population 10 per cent were slaves. (Chroniclers acknowledged that the eventual ending of slavery by the Normans was one of the beneficial consequences of the invasion.)

> At the level of literate and aristocratic society, no country in Europe, between the rise of the barbarian kingdoms and the twentieth century, has undergone so radical a change in so short a time as England experienced after 1066.

Within a matter of decades, William had almost completely replaced the existing English power structure with Normans who owed their allegiance to him. By the time John came to the throne nearly a century and a half later, this forced integration had been so thorough that 'Ethnic distinctions had broken down to the point that one could not know who was English and who was Norman ... the aristocracy of England, descended in large measure from the conquerors, came to identify itself firmly as English.' The assimilation was so complete that by the time of John's battles with his barons, both sides were accusing the other of being anti-English and pro-French. A century and a half after they had forcibly imposed themselves on an alien society, the Anglo-Norman aristocracy was describing itself as the protector of English liberties.

William's successful conquest gave him an empire that stretched from Scotland's eastern coast to the Welsh border, and south to the French province of Maine, which was more than 150 kilometres from the English Channel. His great-grandson Henry II, who became king in 1154, dramatically expanded the size of the realm. Henry claimed large parts of western Ireland, including Dublin, and the Duchy of Brittany in France. Through marriage to Eleanor of Aquitaine, Henry gained the Duchy of Aquitaine, which bordered Spain, and included the towns Bordeaux and Bayonne. Henry also claimed, although he could not fully control, the Duchy of Toulouse, and he even had a degree of control over the independent Scotland, with English garrisons stationed in a number of Scottish castles including in Edinburgh.

The lands acquired by Henry II, the better part of 1,500 kilometres from north to south, have come to be known as the Angevin empire, named after the homeland of Henry's family in Anjou. Anjou was a county based around the city of Angers in the Loire valley in western France. The Angevin kings—Henry II, Richard I, and John—are sometimes also described as the early Plantagenet kings. The term 'Plantagenet' comes from the symbol of Geoffrey's family, the common broom plant, which is a shrub with yellow flowers—in Latin, *Planta genesta*.

Winston Churchill summed up how contemporaries thought of Henry II:

He embodied all their ability, all their energy, and not a little of that passionate, ruthless ferocity which, it was whispered, came from the house of Anjou from no mortal source, but from a union with Satan himself.

The actual control Henry had over his lands should not be overstated. Feudal hierarchies could also apply to monarchs. Some of Henry's territory he ruled as a vassal to the French king, which required regular payment of tribute from Henry to his French overlord. What Henry ruled was a network of allegiances, sometimes loose, sometimes solid, tied together by financial and military relationships. Henry's control was only secure when he visited these regions backed by strong military force: the otherwise powerful local lords rebelled and asserted their independence when his attentions were elsewhere. While the geographic centre of the empire was Anjou in France, Henry's power was based in the Anglo-Norman lands of England and Normandy, where he had the strongest sovereign rights as a lord and landholder. The Angevin empire is a name used by modern historians, not the Angevins' contemporaries. It lacked the sense of unity that would make an empire. The Angevins never imposed a common language, system of government, or currency throughout their realm. Henry and his heirs, however, did regard their vast lands as their heritage—territory which was theirs by right and force.

Travelling across the vast distances of the Angevin empire was a daunting task. An expert rider might be able to travel 50 to 80 kilometres a day if they were able to change horses regularly. Movement was also highly dependent on the weather and the state of the roads. In some areas travellers could use still existing but degrading Roman roads. A rider might be able to travel from London to Toulouse, close to the most southern extent of the empire, within two weeks. The travelling retinue of the monarch was much slower. A medieval court could usually make around 20 kilometres per day. In times of military crisis, the king might be able to move faster. In 1158, Henry II managed to move his army the length of France, from Normandy to Toulouse, in six weeks.

Distance matters because it helps explain the structure of the political arrangements of the medieval world. Communications were only as fast as riders could travel. The Magna Carta was still being distributed across England five weeks after it was sealed. It was thanks to these limitations that the nested jurisdictions of feudal society evolved to maximise political control over large territories that did not have rapid communications or reliable bureaucratic institutions. The institutions—governmental, legal, and military—that gave Roman emperors the capacity to govern vast territory from a central location had disappeared.

Medieval government was simply not capable of defending lives and property against brigands and gangs (there would be no police force in England until the nineteenth century). Security was provided instead by local authorities. Likewise, disputes between the vassals of a lord were adjudicated by the lord's courts. The economic historians Douglass North and Robert Paul Thomas describe feudalism as effectively a system of protection, where one service was exchanged for another service. Key to the enforcement of the system was the notion of 'custom':

> The Western European serf, while born to a contract specifying the kind and extent of his obligations which he could not change without the lord's permission, was in fact also generally protected from arbitrary changes in the terms of the contract by the lord as a consequence of the customs of the manor.

The idea of 'custom' as an institution that balances coercive and potentially exploitative contractual relationships plays an important role in the Magna Carta. The barons claimed that King John had usurped or perverted customary feudal relations. For example, Chapter 16 stated no one was compelled to provide to the king military service or any other sort of services beyond what 'is due' according to the land holdings. What was 'due' was not defined because it was left to custom and past practice to determine. The chapter was an appeal to an unwritten but nonetheless real contractual relationship that had existed in the past and was being violated by John.

In Chapter 48, the Magna Carta refers to the king remedying 'All evil customs connected with forests' and in Chapter 55 to remitting 'All fines which were made with us unjustly and against the law of the land'. In the absence of a definition of what were 'evil customs' and fines imposed 'unjustly', it was custom and practice often going back generations that was relied upon.

In the twenty-first century it is easy to dismiss 'custom' as having little value, much less any virtue as a source of law. At best, customary rules are easily evaded by those who do not value them. At worst, they can enforce regressive and reactionary strictures that prevent society from evolving. We have become used to the idea that all law is statute law—law imposed by rulers or parliaments, and spelled out in legalistic detail. Bruno Leoni, in *Freedom and the Law*, writes that:

> Legislation appears today to be a quick, rational, and far-reaching remedy against every kind of evil or inconvenience, as compared with, say, judicial decisions, the settlement of disputes by private arbiters, conventions, customs, and similar kinds of spontaneous adjustments on the part of individuals.

The idea of custom as a source of law is one well known to anthropologists, who see norms and communal practices as a partly binding constraint on behaviour. When we speak of feudal custom, we are speaking of a legal tradition that evolved out of centuries of specific, individual, and private decisions. The calls to custom in the Magna Carta may seem vague, but they were in fact a rich and present idea in the minds of the medieval English.

The monarchs of England and Normandy had good reason to travel around their lands. But peasants travelled too. The twelfth and thirteenth centuries were a period of urbanisation. In 1086, the Domesday Book—the national survey conducted by William the Conqueror to assess the wealth and population of his new lands—records that no more than 10 per cent of the population lived in one of the 100 urban settlements of the country. By 1300 between 15 and 20 per cent of people lived across 500 settlements that were recognisably towns and cities. In theory, travel for peasants was highly restricted and the labour 'market', such as it was, also was highly restricted. Yet records are replete with cases of individuals housing strangers, contrary to village by-laws. Medieval life could be fluid and migratory. In part this was because of the low quality stock of peasant housing. Timber structures with clay walls and clay floors would rot and degrade, and would not last longer than a generation. Houses were not considered to be permanent structures.

Internal migration, particularly common among the children of the very poor, placed a great deal of pressure on feudal social arrangements. Town life lacked the complex contractual feudal relationships of agrarian life. Town dwellers were free to marry, and did not have to offer service to a lord. The German legal principle *stadtluft macht frei* ('city air makes you free') was also true in England. Peasants in urban areas enjoyed many more liberties than those in rural settings.

The population of England increased substantially in the two centuries after 1066. By the time of the Magna Carta, England's population may have been around three and a half million people. Waves of plague in the fourteenth century then cut the population by half, and England's population growth stagnated until at least the end of the fifteenth century.

This was also a time of relatively rapid economic growth, and the development of a distinct market economy. The traditional idea of the peasant unable to live anything more than a subsistence lifestyle is no longer supportable. Most peasants, in most years, were able to produce a surplus above subsistence which could be traded. It is no coincidence that Sunday became known as market day: petty markets were associated with churchyards, at least until King John regulated them as part of his renewed attention to enforcing canon law. Larger trades were made at the growing number of markets—which, if of large enough size, required a royal charter and a payment to the king.

These markets were a challenge to the feudal economic hierarchies. But they had more political significance than that. Commercial relationships are cooperative relationships, and growing markets led to increasing communication within the peasant classes:

> The pull of distant markets could draw on communities while the established commercial and industrial opportunities within a locale could bring new blood into villages. The market also intensified an awareness of the outside world, bringing with it information, education and a familiarity with new mechanisms, both legal and social. Such experiences were ... features of the peasantry's interaction with politics and religion and, of course, none of these influences on the peasant world acted in isolation or was independent

of the other. Commercial networks and market integration facilitated the spread of political and religious ideas while the market was both a political and a religious issue for all sections of society, including the peasantry. Finally, the interaction of peasants with the market made them substantial figures in the economic life of the country, both as producers and providers of capital.

There were also important changes in technology, economic practice, and infrastructure which facilitated the commercial society. Farmers increasingly replaced oxen with horses. Oxen were better suited for ploughing but horses were more useful for transporting goods to markets. Transport was also eased by a boom in bridge building. Many new bridges were patterned on the new gothic-style cathedrals being constructed around the country. Finally, there was an increase in the use of iron in carts—particularly in the wheels—which made them longer-lasting, and more capable of carrying goods long distances.

One prosaic but significant consequence of increasing market activity was an intense inflation. From the end of the twelfth and throughout the thirteenth century, the price of goods and labour increased dramatically. The prices of some commodities, such as corn and livestock, doubled and in some cases trebled between 1180 and 1220. The inflation perhaps does not seem as severe to our modern eyes, given that this translated to just over 2.75 per cent per year at most. But the importance of inflation is not of its magnitude, but how it relates to the expectations of those it affects.

The causes of this inflation are hotly debated. Most likely, inflation was due to the dramatic expansion of English exports to the continent, particularly wool, finished cloth, tin, and wheat. This resulted in an influx of silver as payment. The number of the silver coins in circulation produced the problem of 'clipping', whereby the edges of coins were clipped to collect the metal they contained. The only coins in circulation were silver pennies. In 1205 John declared that old coins were required to be exchanged for new ones, and it is suspected that an eagerness to dispose of suspect coins in anticipation of a future re-coinage might have contributed to the inflation of the period.

Inflation had significant political and social consequences. It was one of the causes of the contest between John and the barons: 'No landmark in English constitutional history was more clearly brought about by economic change than Magna Carta'. The inflation completely upset the balance of feudal power. Inflation favours those who have to pay debts or dues at a fixed, previously nominated price, set with the assumption that prices would remain stable. The losers of inflation are those who receive what they are owed at a fixed price but have to pay for goods or services at a steadily inflating market rate.

Inflation affected the balance of power across medieval society. Over the course of the twelfth century, money rents had been slowly replacing labour services provided by the vassal to the lord. Inflation meant that landlords who received money in fixed amounts, usually as a result of long term agreements, were worse off in the lead-up to the Magna Carta. There was also an increase in rent paid in the form of labour. Inflation solidified the division between free and unfree labour such that free labour paid rent in money and unfree paid with at least some form of labour.

But these relationships were relatively flexible compared to the relationship between the monarchy and his vassals. Inflation affected the finances of Richard I and John, as they were unable to resort to the sort of techniques used by the barons and other landlords below them—such as directly managing their land—to ameliorate the effects of the inflation. The financial profitability of royal estates declined in the face of inflation. Over time they came to be seen more as sources of patronage rather than revenue. But in the short term, it meant that both Richard and John had to search for new sources of revenue. The problem was their incomes were fixed, but their expenses, particularly mercenaries' wages, were increasing.

> Their failure to raise the income that reached them through the sheriffs' farms to anything like the level demanded by the rise in prices threw the whole burden of their increased expenditure on other forms of revenue. It was not just that John in 1215 had to pay about three times as much as his father fifty years before when he bought food for his household or livestock and corn for his manors; he also had to pay his troops at three times the earlier rates.

> Where a knight could be hired for 8 pennies per day in 1160, the cost was 24 pennies per day by 1220. By comparison, a labourer on a royal building in King John's time was paid 1½ to 2 pennies a day. Military campaigns became more expensive and the price of defending the legacy of Henry II skyrocketed.

CHAPTER
FOUR

THE PRICE OF EMPIRE

The process of succession for medieval monarchies was often complicated and dangerous. Relations frequently warred with each other for the right to the crown. A pretender could easily find supporters since the spoils of victory were enormous. Even if succession was not disputed there was frequently a length of time between the death of one king and the coronation of another. We can get a sense of how dangerous such a period was when a contemporary chronicler noted with astonishment the lack of violence around the ascension of Henry II in 1154:

> The king was dead but kingless England did not lack peace—
> You, Henry, are the first in the world to have performed
> this wonder

Not yet king, not yet present, you nevertheless can do
What a king was unable to do when present ...

When Henry I died in 1135, a brutal war was waged between his daughter Matilda and his nephew Stephen. Both were grandchildren of William the Conqueror. The period came to be known as 'The Anarchy'. The civil war only ended when Stephen recognised Henry II, the son of Matilda and Geoffrey of Anjou, as his heir.

Given how he had become king, Henry II appreciated the need to secure the process for succession after his own death. Fortunately he had some flexibility because, as his empire was effectively a federation, he could distribute different parts of it to different family members. Henry had four legitimate sons (and a number of illegitimate ones). His plan was that the eldest, 'Young Henry', would rule over the core of the empire—Anjou, Normandy, and England. The second son, Richard, would have the lands in the south of France that Eleanor of Aquitaine had brought into the empire on her marriage to Henry. The third son, Geoffrey, was to take Brittany. The plan was that the brothers would be allies, and the empire would remain intact. The youngest son, John, would get money but no land—hence his nickname, John 'Lackland'.

The hopes of Henry II for a smooth succession were forlorn. He ruled from 1154 to 1189 and the last two decades of his life were dominated by the dissension between him and his eldest sons. Tolstoy famously said that all happy families are alike, and that each unhappy family is unhappy in its own way. Angevin family unhappiness was truly unique. The historian W. L. Warren summed up how Henry and his family were regarded:

> passionate and dynamic, with clever minds and strong wills. They had a hot temper which sometimes prejudiced their calculated schemes. They seemed, even to contemporaries, a

little larger than life. Their minds and bodies appeared to work faster than those of normal men. When they conceived anything it was usually on a grand scale; their will matched their conception, and their vast resources were bent to its realisation.

In addition to these strong-willed males there is the dominant figure of Eleanor of Aquitaine. Like her husband and children, Eleanor was larger than life. Because of her family connections throughout Europe, Eleanor was the kingmaker of the Angevin empire. Henry II was a vassal to Louis VII, the king of France. Eleanor had been married to Louis. Henry's son, Young Henry, was married to Louis' daughter. Such marital arrangements were supposed to ensure stability and the mingling of political interests with personal ones, but they instead created a web of divisions and potential divisions that the French kings became adept at exploiting.

The future of the Angevin empire was not just the subject of dispute between Henry's sons—it also produced conflict between his sons and the French kings.

The contest between France and the Angevins is sometimes compared to the Cold War of the middle of the twentieth century. The two superpowers were often on the brink of war. They fought complicated proxy battles through smaller allies, and they held numerous conferences to try to restrain hostilities. But the French-Angevin relationship was more complicated than that between the Soviet Union and the United States.

In 1173, Henry II bequeathed three castles to John that had originally been promised to Young Henry. This enraged Young Henry and his two other brothers. The three eldest brothers and a group of rebel barons launched an uprising against their father supported by King Louis of France. Henry II had not yet even died, and already his sons were fighting a war of succession; the only one who stayed loyal to him was the youngest, John, who was then only seven years old. By July 1174, Henry II managed to suppress the uprising, but the revolt laid the foundations for the unrest that would characterise the rest of his reign.

A second rebellion, in 1183, was sparked when Henry II insisted Richard offer homage to his older brother, Young Henry. Richard refused, and he and Young Henry went to war against each other in Aquitaine. The conflict ended when Young Henry died of a fever in June 1183, aged 28. Henry then had to reset succession plans to give Richard precedence, and had to alter them again in 1186 when Geoffrey died in a tournament in Paris. Louis VII of France had died four years earlier, handing over the French kingdom to his son Philip II. Exploiting the Angevin family divisions, the new French king allied with Richard to launch a third rebellion against Henry in 1189. It was during this campaign that Henry II, old and weary at 56, succumbed to illness and died. Legend has it that as Henry lay dying, father and son reconciled. As Henry gave the kiss of peace to Richard he uttered to his son, 'May the Lord spare me until I have taken vengeance on you'. Henry never did get his revenge. On Henry's death in July 1189, Richard—behind whom John had thrown his support at the final hour—was the undisputed ruler of the Angevin empire.

One result of such attrition of heirs of Henry II was that the Angevin empire passed intact to Richard. With his possessions relatively secure, Richard turned his attention to the Holy Land. His father Henry had been encouraged to go on crusade as penance for the murder of Archbishop Thomas Becket, killed in 1170 probably on Henry's orders. But Henry had a sense of caution, and declined to leave on crusade. Richard was less careful. In 1187, Jerusalem had been captured by Saladin. In response, Richard set off on the Third Crusade in 1189 to take back the Holy Land.

Thanks to his crusading endeavours, Richard I is now remembered as one of the great kings of medieval England. Yet Richard was absent from England for most of his reign. Indeed, he spent just six months in England during his decade on the throne. Richard left for the Crusades shortly after becoming king. His army made many gains but failed to recapture Jerusalem in 1192. Having concluded a peace treaty with Saladin, he then sought to return to friendly territory but became shipwrecked in Aquileia in northern Italy. While taking a dangerous land-route back home, he was captured by the Duke of Austria, Leopold V, who had become an opponent of Richard because of a quarrel while on crusade. Leopold later handed Richard over to the Holy Roman Emperor, Henry VI, who was similarly angry at Richard over his support of a coup in Sicily, and demanded a ransom for his release of 100,000 marks. As Richard's regent in England, Eleanor approved a massive 25 per cent tax on all moveable property to meet the ransom—the highest rate of tax in the history of medieval England. The Cistercian order, whose members had taken a vow of poverty, were required to hand over the year's wool clip. The sum was raised and Richard was freed in February 1194.

For an apparently great king this was an ignominious legacy. In Richard's absence, Philip of France had allied with John and overrun Normandy. Richard reconquered Normandy and spent the last years of his life in France fighting the French king. In March 1199, he was hit in the shoulder by an arrow while besieging a small castle in Aquitaine held by a rebellious viscount. The wound turned gangrenous and he died. The sole legitimate surviving heir of Henry II was John. He was 32 years old.

Angevin dynastic dramas left their mark on the government of England. Richard had been little interested in his English possessions, and appears to have looked upon them primarily as a source of revenue to support his conquests. England was a financial asset, rather than a political one. While on crusade, he handed over practical power in England to Archbishop Hubert Walter, acknowledged at that time and since as an able administrator. As Archbishop of Canterbury, Walter was head of both the English church and of the secular government—a successful attempt to reduce the conflicts between the church and the state that had plagued Henry II and would frustrate John.

One of Walter's main jobs was to raise enough revenue to support Richard's wars in France. As the twelfth century progressed, it became increasingly obvious that these usual sources of revenue were not sufficient to support the rising cost of military ventures overseas. Nor was revenue particularly reliable:

> The machinery for collecting the income was inefficient. It was impossible for the exchequer to compel the prompt payment of dues. The rolls are full of debts which have run on for years. Instead of insisting on the payment of the full sum as a government would do to-day, arrangements were often made with a debtor to pay a certain amount each year till the debt was discharged. A considerable part of the revenue was thus continually in arrears.

The monarchy was forced to rely on irregular revenue—the special tallages, tithes, and scutages which could be imposed at the monarch's or lord's discretion. Both Henry II in England and King Louis in France had imposed a one-off national tax on property in 1166 to fund the Crusades in the Holy Land, at a rate of two pennies to every pound's worth of all property (there were 240 pennies in a pound). Despite the apparent success of this new national tax, Henry II continued to subsist on traditional feudal revenues for the better part of the next twenty years. His next attempt to levy a national tax was made in 1185, but by far the largest was the infamous 'Saladin Tithe' of 1188. Initiated shortly before his death, it had originally been requested by the papacy to support the reconquest of Jerusalem after its capture by Saladin. The tax was levied at the rate of one tenth of all income and one tenth of the value of all personal property. The tax applied to all those, clergy and laymen, who had not chosen to join the Crusade—in part because Henry had wanted to give an incentive for people to fight. Taxpayers assessed their liabilities themselves and swore an oath that their calculations were accurate. If anyone was suspected of not paying sufficient tax, their neighbours were coerced into doing the assessment for the government.

When the Saladin Tithe was levied in France it sparked such serious protests from the clergy it had to be rescinded by King Philip. Outrage was somewhat less overt in England, but the Saladin Tithe was still a bitterly resented tax. Few in France or England could object with a war to defend the Holy Land against the Muslims. Yet even for Henry II's admirers, the Saladin Tithe was a black mark against his name. Gerald of Wales sympathised with the cause but was angry about the burden of the tax:

> How I wish that they had set out on this wearisome but glorious journey with followers who were fewer in number, but more effective, and men who were pleasing in God's sight, rather than that, having not such followers, they should, in this critical struggle, boast of having their treasuries full of vast sums of money, money gathered indiscriminately from every quarter …

Indeed, Gerald characterised Henry's death as God's punishment for such an extraordinary exaction.

When he came to power, Richard benefited handsomely from the funds raised by the Saladin Tithe. Yet taxes had to be raised again to finance Richard's journey to the Holy Land. Then they had to be raised even further in order to finance his extremely steep ransom.

Henry II had only imposed scutage on his vassals once every four to five years. Richard increased the frequency to once every three years. Once John came to the throne, he levied scutage every eighteen months. Furthermore, the rate of scutage imposed doubled in the time between Henry II and John.

Economic theory and practical experience suggest these taxes would have been a heavy drain on the economy, as well as a heavy burden for those who paid them. Gerald of Wales was not the only person in England to resent tithes, even if he supported the cause for which they were raised. These taxes were a net drain on the British economy. A war in the Holy Land is unlikely to boost the productive capacity of the economy, and Richard's ransom was a direct money transfer from British subjects to a foreign monarch. It is difficult to be certain, given the limited available historical records, but it is highly likely that the extraordinary taxes imposed by Richard had depleted the economy and decreased the amount of money that John was able to extract from his subjects.

There was an important and novel aspect of the large-scale taxes of 1166, 1188, and 1193. In each instance, the monarch or their representatives sought the council of an assembly of barons and the clergy. In the case of the ransom, this was not at all necessary according to feudal custom—a lord was well within his traditional rights to levy his vassals to pay a ransom. Nevertheless, 'a king's ransom was quite exceptional, and the sum demanded for Richard's so large, that the securing of some form of consent must have seemed only prudent.'

The heavy taxation of Richard's reign led to at least one serious rebellion in 1196. Like all other urban centres in post-Conquest England, London was growing rapidly. At the time of the Magna Carta, it had population of around 40,000, a figure that perhaps doubled by 1300. London, like all other towns and cities, paid a lump sum tax directly to the king: it was collected internally within the city before being handed to the royal treasury. The city had won a number of privileges over the course of the thirteenth century—for instance, it won the right to have its own mayor, and administer itself relatively independently, including having responsibility for the levying of its own taxes. Taxes were collected by aldermen who apparently levied higher rates on wealthier people.

The rebellion was sparked by a dispute over how the burden of taxation should be distributed. The heavier tax burden imposed by Richard led to disputes within the city about what the rich had to pay. The chronicler Richard of Hoveden claimed that 'more frequently than usual, in consequence of the king's captivity and other accidents, aids to no small amount were imposed upon them, and the rich men, sparing their own purses, wanted the poor to pay everything'. In stepped a charismatic Londoner, William Fitz Osbert, who was 'moderately educated [but] unusually eloquent' and with a 'sharp mind'. His nickname was 'Longbeard', referring to that feature which made him stand out in the London assemblies and folk meetings that constituted the governance of the city. These gatherings allowed him to gain a great deal of prominence within London without having any formal title or position. Styling himself the 'advocate of the poor', Fitz Osbert objected to the share of the tax burden being borne by the poorer classes. In fact, he probably also represented not just the city's destitute but the middle classes—traders, manufacturers, and small property owners—who were not the wealthiest but had sufficient property to be profitably taxed.

Fitz Osbert disrupted meetings and organised resistance to the city aldermen. He held meetings himself. There were claims that he had 52,000 supporters. This was certainly an exaggeration (it would have been more than the population of London itself), nevertheless such rumours give us some indication of the depth of feeling and the level of his support in the city. A riot was attributed to his rhetoric.

Fitz Osbert appealed to Richard for a more reasonable tax burden, although that appears to have come to little. The appeal to the king certainly did not prevent Hubert Walter from deciding that the unrest had gone too far. Walter sent two loyal Londoners along with some armed men to arrest the rebel. Fitz Osbert and his supporters managed to kill one of the men, and, seeking sanctuary, fled to the tower of St Mary-le-Bow church. Walter sent more soldiers into the city, and set the church on fire. Fitz Osbert escaped the church and was arrested. After a time in the Tower of London and a trial, Fitz Osbert was made an example of. He was dragged 'through the centre of the city to the elms, his flesh was demolished and spread all over the pavement and, fettered with a chain, he was hanged that same day on the elms with his associates and died'.

The barons' rebellion against John was a revolt of the rich. The story of Fitz Osbert demonstrates that it was not just the rich who felt the heavy weight of Angevin revenue raising.

CHAPTER FIVE

THE FOULNESS OF JOHN

King John has come down through history as one of the most incompetent and most tyrannical English monarchs—a potent and dangerous combination. The influential nineteenth century historian William Stubbs gave John his modern legacy when he penned these acerbic words in his *Constitutional History of England*:

> He was the very worst of all our kings: a man whom no oaths could bind, no pressure of conscience, no consideration of policy, restrain from evil; a faithless son, a treacherous brother, an ungrateful master; to his people a hated tyrant. Polluted with every crime that could disgrace a man; false to every obligation that should bind a king,

he had lost half his inheritance by sloth, and ruined and desolated the rest.

John's reputation was even worse among his contemporaries. Matthew Paris wrote that 'Foul as it is, Hell itself is defiled by the foulness of John'. Over the centuries the standing of John has waxed and waned. In the age of Elizabeth, John was praised for having stood up to the Pope. In Shakespeare's play *King John*, John is portrayed sympathetically as he berates a papal legate:

> What earthly name to interrogatories
> Can task the free breath of a sacred king?
> Thou canst not, cardinal, devise a name
> So slight, unworthy, and ridiculous,
> To charge me to an answer, as the pope.

The break of the English Church from Rome under Henry VIII ensured there was a market for dramatic depictions of anti-papal theatrics. Other plays—such as *The Troublesome Reign*, which Shakespeare may have derived much of his King John from—are more explicit examples of John as a proto-Protestant hero. It's often been noted that Shakespeare's *King John* makes no mention of the Magna Carta. In Tudor England there was a reluctance to make mention of an event which attempted to control a rapacious over-mighty monarch.

John was born in December 1166. Like all children of nobles at the time, he was not brought up by his parents. He spent his first few years at the Fontevraud Abbey in Anjou. It may have been intended he join the clergy. Nevertheless, John accompanied his father when Henry fought to defend his empire against John's three older brothers. One can only imagine how the experience of his siblings warring against his father shaped his character.

John was well looked after by Richard. Richard knew that his royal power was dependent on the legacy left to him by Henry II, and granted John virtual autonomy over large swathes of British territory, including Nottinghamshire, Derbyshire, Lancaster, Cornwall, Devon, Dorset, and Somerset. One historian has observed that 'At no time since the Conquest, probably, had a subject been allowed to exercise control over so vast a territory … Men had occasionally been granted enormous fiefs, to be sure, but the king had always taken care that the lands should be widely scattered rather than contiguous.'

Yet while Richard was on the continent and on crusade, John had unsuccessfully tried to usurp Richard's authority in England. Richard was contemptuous: 'My brother John is not the man to conquer a country if there is a single person able to make the slightest resistance to his attempts.' John tearfully apologised and Richard patronisingly told the 27-year-old, 'You are a child. You have had bad companions.' John had a reputation as a weak military leader, in contrast to his crusading brother and empire-building father. Later chroniclers dubbed John 'Softsword'.

When Richard died the norms of succession had not been entrenched to the extent that it was clear who should become king. Although Richard did have an illegitimate son, it seems Richard preferred John to be his successor. Another claimant was Arthur, the twelve-year-old son of Richard and John's deceased brother Geoffrey. There was no clear order of precedence. Arthur was supported by Philip II of France. John was the English candidate. Eleanor supported John, suspecting Arthur of being hostile to the Angevin family. The situation quickly escalated into an armed dispute, as John sought to take his lands by force before Arthur could do so. John's hold on England and Aquitaine was secure, but it was not secure over the rest of the empire. Nobles in Anjou, Brittany and Maine aligned themselves with Arthur. Nevertheless, a short war between Philip II and John ended with John holding the upper hand. An uncomfortable truce was settled in 1200. John was lord of Anjou and Brittany, Arthur was his vassal in those lands, and both were vassals of the French crown. Parts of Normandy were ceded to France.

The truce only lasted two years. What happened subsequently was a product of John's political ineptitude and cruelty. Time and time again John would win strategic victories but undermine those victories through pettiness and brutality. In August 1200, John decided he wanted to marry Isabella of Angoulême, whose family was strategically located in Aquitaine. He divorced the wife he had been allocated by Henry II two decades earlier, and took up with Isabella. There was a complication, however. Isabella was already engaged to a noble, Hugh le Brun, whose family held strategically significant lands in Normandy near the French border. While Isabella's links to Aquitaine ought to have worked to his favour, John managed to turn this marriage from a political triumph into a political catastrophe. Instead of attempting to appease le Brun, he challenged him to trial by battle with champions. John's contempt drove le Brun and his allies into rebellion and the arms of Philip II.

The relationship between John and Philip rapidly deteriorated until 1202, when it escalated into open warfare. Despite John's reputation for military feebleness, he managed some victories against Philip. The most remarkable of these victories was John's sudden march from a defensive position in Normandy to relieve his mother, caught up in a siege at Mirabeau by the forces of Arthur, who was now sixteen years old. John took Arthur's forces completely by surprise, attacking before they had eaten breakfast and capturing a large number of high-born rebels, including Arthur himself. This was an unambiguous military victory.

Yet John managed to lose the political benefits of his military achievement. John mistreated many of the powerful and prominent nobles he had captured. Twenty-two of them died. In thirteenth century Europe, this was seen as well beyond the rules of war. The true barbarity was his treatment of Arthur. John was not as willing to tolerate rivals. On his capture Arthur was imprisoned in Rouen castle in Normandy. Arthur disappeared in 1203. What actually happened to him is a mystery. The traditional story is that John sent men to blind and castrate Arthur, but they were stopped by Hubert de Burgh who felt sympathy for the boy. One legend from the time is that John himself murdered Arthur.

> [S]ome time after Arthur's imprisonment, the King came much intoxicated to Rouen Castle; and having murdered him there with his own hand, he caused a great stone to be fastened to the corpse, and had it thrown into the river.

Regardless of the truth, it was widely believed that John was responsible for Arthur's death.

The collapse of the Angevin empire came swiftly. The French king, Philip, was able to capitalise on the alienation of John's allies in Normandy and Anjou. Over the course of 1204, Philip swept up Normandy. The death of Eleanor of Aquitaine the same year loosened the bonds between southern nobles and John's family. In short order, John lost the core of the Angevin empire, Anjou and Maine. Aquitaine was then invaded by Alfonso VIII, the King of Castile. The only territory remaining in John's control was Gascony, a small area on the Atlantic coast around Bordeaux. (The Hundred Years War between England and France was sparked in 1337 when the French king attempted to claim that area of Aquitaine, still held by the English monarch.)

By the end of 1204 John had lost Henry II's inheritance,

and the relationship between Normandy and England, forged by William the Conqueror, was severed. For the rest of his reign John was engaged in a futile effort to recapture the territories he had lost. This was a time where kingly virtues were tested against romantic tales like King Arthur. The narrative account of the King Arthur legend by Geoffrey of Monmouth was published around 1138. But John had all the Angevin passion without the charm. As one historian writes, John 'could be courteous. He could give. But there was always something false and calculating about it'.

John's reputation was further damaged by the fact that the dead Arthur was named after the Arthur of legend. Nor did it help that his brother Richard had been such a great, crusading military leader. This was an era when the chivalric code was being developed—informal rules of conduct that combined Christian conduct, honour, and military prowess. John's loss of Normandy and the end of the Angevin empire meant that he would never meet these standards. Historians today argue that John was a highly skilled administrator. But that was of little interest to chroniclers. What mattered in a king was his military virtues, not his bureaucratic ones.

After the loss of his empire John faced a double political and financial crisis. Losing his ancestral lands was a political crisis. Medieval kings were meant to win wars and territory, not lose them. But with the loss of Normandy, John didn't have the economic base to raise the revenue to launch a campaign to reclaim what he had lost.

It is estimated that when John came to the throne in 1199 his financial resources were around half of what was available to the French king. When John lost Normandy in 1204 his fiscal position became even worse. The financial damage of continental war had already started to bite before John's reign. Louis and his son Philip had undergone a revolution in administration that meant they were steadily increasing their financial resources. New finances allowed the French monarchs to live in greater luxury, but it also bought new mercenaries and funds which could be distributed among supporters.

Richard had staved off the military consequences of the financial disparity by soaking the tax base to its limit. The funds for Richard's defence of Normandy were devoted to castle construction and fortification, but with the result that the region was impoverished. Building castles had short-term military advantages, but John came to inherit a much depleted resource base. 'John's financial problems were indeed of Richard's making.'

It was this destruction of the tax base that gave John's efforts at revenue-raising their sense of oppressive desperation. John started to embrace one of the most powerful tools in his taxation armoury: the tax on all personal property. In 1201, drawing on a precedent set by Richard, John levied a tax of a fortieth of the value of all moveable property. In 1203 he had levied a tax of a seventh on the moveable property of barons and earls. Henry II had imposed the discretionary feudal tax—the 'tallage'—on the lands and towns he directly controlled just five times over the course of 30 years. By contrast, Richard had imposed a tallage every year between 1194 and 1199. John did so four times between 1202 and 1206.

Even with the withdrawal from the continent and a period of relative peace, John's fiscal desires were undiminished. The taxes early in his reign were test runs for the much more significant Thirteenth tax in 1207. It was one of John's most controversial taxes. It was a truly national tax: imposed on lay and clerical assets, as well as feudal and non-feudal property alike. John seemed to have known that this tax was a larger imposition than any previous tax, and proclaimed it had the authority of 'the common counsel and assent of our council'—that is, he implied he had the approval of the barons. In January 1207, the levy had indeed been discussed in a meeting of nobles convened at short notice where the tax was grudgingly accepted.

Nevertheless, any goodwill engendered by the consultative approach to tax approval was squandered as a result of the oppressive manner in which the Thirteenth was levied. It involved individuals swearing oaths to special justices rather than self-assessing as they had in the past. The agents of the state spidering out across the country gave the distinct appearance of a more formal—and regular—extraordinary taxation program than the English crown had imposed in the past. It was also matched by unprecedented compliance penalties. John clearly expected resistance to his tax. Tax evaders were to have all their property confiscated and they were to be imprisoned at the king's pleasure. This was not an idle threat. In the north there was widespread evasion. Three men were imprisoned and the Archbishop of York fled the country.

Why was the Thirteenth so unpopular? While it was smaller than some levies which had been imposed in the past—recall that Richard took a quarter of all property to fund his ransom—the Thirteenth was not levied in a time of crisis, but of peace. Custom dictated that extraordinary taxation was intended for extraordinary times. The fortieth in 1201 had been imposed for the service of the Holy Lands. The seventh in 1203 had been imposed for the defence of Angevin Europe. But in 1207, England was at peace. John wanted to retake his continental possessions but the 1207 tax was just to build up his revenues.

The widespread resistance to the Thirteenth meant that John could never again levy a national tax on moveables. Instead, he began 'asset stripping'. John aggressively exploited every feudal source of revenue available and he sold what he could with little regard for the economic consequences of his actions. For instance, in 1204 he introduced general customs duties on imports and exports (under the feudal arrangements, duties were originally levied by the ports themselves, who paid the monarch for the privilege). The customs duties had to be removed by the 1206 peace treaty with Philip that established free trade, but by 1210, John was making efforts to re-establish tariffs.

Over time, the more taxes John imposed, the less money they raised. Resistance to taxation involves evasion long before it manifests into armed revolt. Heavier scutages were being paid by fewer and fewer of those who were liable. As one history of premodern taxation notes, 'evasion, delays and resistance by those liable to pay and those concerned in the collection of scutage resulted in diminishing returns and, on each occasion, an increasing discrepancy between the amount put in charge and that actually raised.'

John's problems did not only stem from his unsuccessful wars and arbitrary taxation. He was unlucky to confront one of history's most ambitious popes and one of the great figures of the High Middle Ages, Pope Innocent III. Born as Lotario dei Conti di Segni in the small town of Gavignano near Rome, he was elected at the age of 37, on the same day that his predecessor Celestine died. By comparison Celestine had been the astonishingly old age of 85 when he was elected pope. Young and ambitious, Innocent was also very bright. He was, in the words of one of his modern biographers, a man of 'many virtues and few vices'.

Innocent came to the head of the Western Church at a time when the medieval papacy was at its most influential. Since the reforms of Pope Gregory VII, who had died in 1085, Rome had been expanding its influence over the rulers of western Christendom. The ultimate aim of their program was to constrain the power of secular kings and concentrate the power of the church in Rome. England had presented a problem. While the French king, Louis VII, had been a model of a Christian monarch, Henry II had proved stubborn and independent. Early in his reign, John showed signs of being much like his father.

Conflict between the pope and King John came to a head over the appointment of the Archbishop of Canterbury. In theory, bishops were elected by a council of the cathedral's resident monks—the cathedral chapter. But episcopal power was as divided and complex as any other power structure in the feudal world. The king also had influence through the right he claimed to approve the final choice of bishop. Meanwhile, the pope had a right to intervene in disputed elections, and it was the assertion of this papal prerogative which facilitated the growing influence of the post-Gregory church over secular monarchies. In practice, when there was a vacancy for a bishop, there could be a royal candidate, a papal one, and a cathedral chapter candidate, with the final decision determined by the vagaries of feudal and broader European politics.

Richard's English administrator, Hubert Walter, had become Archbishop of Canterbury in 1193, and remained in that position until he died in 1205. The position was one of the two highest in the English church (the other being the archbishopric of York), and was a powerful countervailing force to the power of the monarchy—as was made dramatically manifest in the contest between Henry II and Thomas Becket. John's difficulties with the pope began when, following Hubert's death, John wanted to appoint the Bishop of Norwich, John de Gray, to the now vacant archbishopric. De Gray had been in John's service before he ascended to the throne and was active in secular politics: he had been Hubert Walter's deputy when the latter was Lord Chancellor.

As was often the case, however, the election was contested. The cathedral chapter chose an in-house candidate: their sub-prior, Reginald. On top of this, the bishops of the province of Canterbury claimed they had the right to elect Walter's successor. Suffice to say, when no agreement could be reached, each party appealed to Rome. Innocent put a hold on any candidate throughout 1206 as each party sought to force the issue. Eventually, Innocent made his own decision. He appointed to the position Stephen Langton, an English-born theologian teaching at the University of Paris. Langton was consecrated by Innocent III as Archbishop of Canterbury in June 1207, and the pope wrote to John that 'to fight against God and the Church in this cause for which St. Thomas, that glorious martyr and archbishop, recently shed his blood, would be dangerous for you'.

John's reaction was swift and aggressive. Both John and his brother Richard regarded clerical positions as their gift. Early in John's reign five of eight bishops elected were members of his extended family, and another two were his close supporters. Feeling he had a customary right to choose the archbishopric, John refused to accept Innocent's consecration of Langton for Canterbury. He prevented Langton entering England and seized property belonging to local Italian clerics.

Innocent had a few tools at his disposal to get John to back down—diplomatic and spiritual. His first response to John's intransigence was to place England under a papal interdict. An interdict prevented the church from carrying out religious services. There could be no masses, marriages, or religious burials—only baptisms and the confessions of the dying were permitted. Innocent had threatened Richard with an interdict if he did not make peace with France and support the crusades in 1198, then threatened John with an interdict over Normandy in 1203 when he mistreated two senior clerics.

Unsurprisingly, John saw the interdict as an opportunity for more expropriation. As Gerald of Wales said, this was a double blow for the clergy. First they were prevented from divine service, and then their property was confiscated. John ordered the confiscation of 'all the lands and goods of abbots, priors, and all religious, and the clergy of [those dioceses] who do not wish to celebrate divine services.' The justification for this confiscation was similar to the traditional custodianship of lands while nobles reached adulthood, with John earning all the revenue from those lands in the interim. But the king's financial intentions were obvious. He offered clergy a choice: pay to recover their lands or go into exile. Needless to say, while it was intended to punish John, the interdict turned out to be extremely profitable for English revenues. It may have even postponed John's day of reckoning, relieving the fiscal burden on the barons for as long as church revenues could be expropriated.

After a year of negotiation over Langton's position, Innocent excommunicated John in November 1209. At first John attempted to negotiate his way out of the excommunication, but then he had a masterstroke. Reasoning that he would have to eventually back down on the interdict and excommunication, and fearing a French invasion supported by the pope, he decided that rather than just accede to Langton's position, he would fully submit himself to the papacy. In May 1213 he not only accepted many of Innocent's terms, he also offered England and Ireland as a fiefdom of the Vatican. John would provide the papacy with feudal dues, and the papacy would provide John with political support. John swore to defend the church, offered his fealty to the bishops, and begged forgiveness. This surprise penitence turned Innocent from being John's opponent into one of his strongest supporters almost overnight—a rare political victory for the king.

REBELLION

In many ways John's behaviour as king was no worse than that of his father Henry or his brother Richard. John's problem was he had lost the family empire. His efforts to regain that empire drove the barons, and the country, to the crisis that culminated in the Magna Carta.

One of the most astute modern historians of the period, Nicholas Vincent, has written perceptively:

> Magna Carta was a response not to one particular king or set of circumstances but to an entire tradition of 'Angevin' kingship. There is no doubt that John was a bad king. His badness, however, was an inherited family characteristic. In many ways, it was his failure to do bad as successfully

and with such impunity as either his father or his elder brother that led him to the surrenders that Magna Carta embodied.

Tales of John's cruelty were used by the barons to justify their rebellion. One of John's most notorious acts was against William de Braose, formerly his close ally. After John had captured his nephew Arthur in 1203 the king handed custody of Arthur to de Braose. Years later stories emerged that the wife of de Braose, Maud, had suggested she knew that John had ordered Arthur's murder. When John found out about Maud's comments he imprisoned her and her son and starved them to death. De Braose fled the country and died in exile in France.

The story of the relationship between John and one his most important barons, Eustace de Vesci, reveals a great deal about how John conducted politics, and how he lost the allegiance of so many of the barons. In the years before Runnymede, Eustace de Vesci plotted the assassination of John. Later he was one of the barons who forced the king to agree to the Magna Carta, and supported the French invasion of England.

Eustace de Vesci came from good Conquest stock. One of his forebears had been a knight in the army of William the Conqueror. Eustace was one of the most powerful lords in England's north, with extensive holdings in Northumberland and Yorkshire. His most prominent possession, Alnwick Castle, still stands today a few kilometres from the English border with Scotland and from the North Sea. Over the centuries the castle has been substantially modified and extended. Today it is the home of the Duke of Northumberland. It is open to the public and was used as the location for Hogwarts school in the *Harry Potter* films.

The de Vesci family was well known for their military exploits. They had fought and been killed in the Holy Land, across France, and throughout the British Isles. The de Vescis were 'sword-bearing lords who upheld the ideals of the chivalrous society perhaps more effectively than most. Their merit as men of blood affirmed their standing among their peers, and simultaneously validated their privileged role as leaders of society.' As a young man, Eustace had accompanied King Richard to the Holy Land. He would be killed in 1216 fighting John's successor, Henry III, when he made the mistake of raising his helmet and was killed instantly by a crossbow bolt to the forehead.

Militaristic though he might have been, Eustace has been described as 'cautious, even parsimonious'. He was careful with his fortune, and avoided the fiscal entanglements typical of leading barons of the time. He only ever had one major piece of litigation in the king's courts, over a manor in Rotherham, which was settled by a duel which he won.

Eustace was also wealthy enough to have to pay 1,300 marks in relief, a huge sum, when he came of age in 1191. He was also deeply involved in the growing commercial development of thirteenth century England. He obtained, and profited from, a port licence granted to the town of Alnmouth, where the Aln River meets the North Sea.

In addition to their massive land holdings, their proximity to Scotland made the de Vescis an essential part of royal power in the north. Eustace himself had married Margaret, an illegitimate daughter of William the Lion, King of the Scots. The family was deeply intertwined in English as well as Scottish politics. The imposing Alnwick Castle had held off a Scottish invasion in 1174. When Eustace was killed, he was standing beside his brother-in-law, Alexander II of Scotland. Eustace de Vesci's lands and connections made the division between him and King John significant.

In the years after the Magna Carta, a story gained currency which attempted to explain why Eustace de Vesci rebelled against John. According to the tale, John attempted to seduce de Vesci's wife. One chronicler of the early fourteenth century, Walter of Guisborough, even argued the attempted seduction was the main cause of the barons' revolt. Walter wrote that one day, while the two men were having dinner, Eustace was convinced by John to give the king his ring. The conniving John immediately sent the ring to Margaret at home, with a note purporting to be from her husband, warning her that he was on his deathbed and she should come at once. A distressed Margaret hurried towards London, where John was waiting for her. But by coincidence, Eustace came across her on the road as he was travelling north, and recognising John's plan, sent a common woman in her place. This counter-ruse was enough to trick John. The king had the unfortunate habit of bragging about his exploits. But when he boasted about his seduction to de Vesci, the baron responded: 'It is not so, King, for you have not had my wife; but in her place you have had a horrible prostitute and washer-woman.' He was threatened by the angry king and de Vesci fled to the north of England. 'Many of the magnates joined him', wrote Walter, 'and particularly those whose wives the King had violated; they rose up with one mind against the king.'

An equally unlikely explanation for the rebellion was offered by some chroniclers concerning one of Eustace's key allies: Robert Fitzwalter, the lord of Dunmow Castle in Essex and Baynard's Castle in London. Fitzwalter was related—either by blood or by marriage—to many of the other powerful magnates in England at the time. Though described by one chronicler as 'one of the greatest men in England, and one of the most powerful', his life story paints an image of an inconsistent and sometimes aggressive man, of frequently dubious motives. In 1203, while John was waging war in France, Fitzwalter and his close friend, Saer de Quincy, were placed in charge of the important fortress of Vaudreuil in Normandy. Though the fortress was well defended and supplied, for an unknown reason, the two men surrendered it to King Philip of France without exchanging a blow, provoking accusations of disloyalty and cowardice. Both were kept hostage in France, and Fitzwalter's cousin was left with the gruelling task of raising a ransom. Unlike de Vesci, Fitzwalter was frequently involved in litigation and land speculation.

One later tradition says that John made the mistake of also trying to seduce Fitzwalter's daughter, Matilda, who had married Geoffrey de Mandeville, the son of King John's chief minister. The tradition claims that the attempted seduction drove Fitzwalter to rebellion. Though this story is perhaps even more questionable than the story of Eustace and Margaret, in the realm of legend it has an interesting coda. The historical Matilda found herself fictionally recast as Maid Marion in seventeenth century versions of the Robin Hood story. A play based on the story, *King John and Matilda*, was first performed in 1655.

The conclusion of his alliance with the pope in 1213 gave John the political capital to pursue the recapture of the territories he had lost in France. He forged diplomatic ties with nobles from the Low Countries and the Holy Roman Emperor, prepared for a new large-scale call on feudal dues, and requisitioned an army. Yet while he was rebuilding his financial base and aligning foreign allies for a war in Normandy, John's arbitrary style of government was destabilising his position with the barons.

In the year before John's settlement with the pope a group of barons had formed a plot to assassinate the king. Both Eustace de Vesci and Robert Fitzwalter were involved. The plan was apparently to have John murdered while he was on campaign in Wales, or, alternatively, to abandon him in the middle of a battle against the Welsh and let the enemy take care of the rest. According to some theories, they had already chosen their preferred monarch to replace John: Simon de Montfort, the French nobleman and leading crusader, and the father of his more famous namesake.

But the plot was discovered. John's response was swift. He immediately demanded hostages and the surrender of castles from those he suspected were involved. For instance, the Northumbrian baron Richard de Umfreville had to surrender Prudhoe Castle, along with his four sons, and pledge that his life and all his possessions were forfeit if he was ever convicted of treason. Eustace de Vesci fled to Scotland, and Robert Fitzwalter to France. John confiscated their castles and sent loyal troops north, where the baronial opposition was strongest. One consequence of the internal conflict was that the planned 1213 invasion of Normandy had to be delayed. John had summoned an invasion army from his vassals in August, but the belligerent northern barons refused to participate. John nevertheless took his shell of an invasion force as far as Jersey before he turned around and went back England. When he returned, he forged an agreement with the northern barons to protect the 'ancient liberties' of the north—an arrangement which held off the rebellion for a short time.

One of the conditions of the settlement with Innocent III was that John restore to power those who had plotted against him a year earlier. The plotters appear to have convinced the pope that their fight against the king was as worthy as the pope's fight against him. Eustace de Vesci and Robert Fitzwalter returned to England. De Vesci and those who held land in the north of England refused to give support for the king's French campaigns. The northern barons, in particular, had very little stake in the planned Angevin re-establishment. Few had any interests in Normandy. They were more likely to have ties with Scotland than France.

John finally launched his war in France to claim back his lost territories in February 1214. It was initially a great success. John himself went south to Poitiers and sent a force commanded by William Longespée, his half-brother and an illegitimate son of Henry II, to the Low Countries. Longespée was to attack Normandy from the east, and John from the south, splitting the French forces and picking them off one at a time. John captured castle after castle, including the city of Nantes. In June 1214, he found himself once again holding Angers, the capital of his ancestral Anjou. This was to be the high point of the invasion. The French regained the strategic momentum, and John, unable to gain the support of the barons of Anjou, retreated south and was effectively defeated.

John was not present at the battle which truly doomed his 1214 campaign. Longespée had joined forces with an army headed by the Holy Roman Emperor, Otto IV. On 27 July 1214 the joint army drew up against the army of the French King Philip at Bouvines, about 85 kilometres west of Brussels. The combined forces of the English and Otto IV outnumbered the French: 25,000 soldiers compared to 15,000. It was a resounding victory for the smaller force. Philip won the battle in just three hours, capturing Longespée and nearly killing Otto. Philip turned his army south to meet John, and as the English king's allies deserted him, John settled a peace agreement with Philip. By October 1214, John was back in England, and the efforts of ten years of preparation for war had resulted in dismal failure.

The result of the Battle of Bouvines was to establish French dominance on the continent and to destroy any dream of re-establishing Angevin supremacy in mainland Europe. John's strategy for the 1214 campaign was actually very well conceived but for one critical detail: it relied too heavily on communication between John's army in the south and the German-English army in the north. The invasion strategy might very well have succeeded, giving him the European dominance that Philip now came to enjoy. It was said that the students of Paris sang and danced for seven days when they heard the result at Bouvines. The battle has entered French history as one of the central moments in the development of the French nation. Had John triumphed at Bouvines, the battle could well have had the same legacy for a cross-channel English empire. Instead, as it was, John returned to England humiliated and vulnerable, having devoted vast financial resources to his failed campaign.

John had not even landed back in England when the barons' rebellion passed the point of no return. In October 1214, at around the time John landed back in England, a group of barons met at Bury St Edmunds in Suffolk, where it seems they resolved to use force unless John swore to abide by the coronation charter of Henry I from 1100. Henry had promised to 'end all the oppressive practices which have been an evil presence in England' and, importantly, he committed to maintain the laws of Edward the Confessor and to take 'advice' from his barons. Of course, Edward was an Anglo-Saxon king, not a Norman one. The Normans might have conquered England but it was the Anglo-Saxon legal heritage that Henry promised to uphold. Henry's coronation oath is just fourteen chapters and around 500 words long, and its parallels with the Magna Carta are clear. Henry promised to limit the payments for inheritances, regulate his control of marriages and dowries, and specified that the penalties against barons who committed crimes would be 'appropriate'. Henry's oath came to be called the 'Charter of Liberties' and in John's time was well-known to both nobles and churchmen. The coronation oath of Henry I provided a model for the barons as the shape of the Magna Carta came to be formed.

Hearing of this meeting, John hurried with a show of force to Suffolk, accompanied by nobles who, still maintaining outward fealty to the king, were in fact participants in the baronial opposition.

The next step for the barons was to present John with their demands. They did this at London in January 1215. Provocatively, the barons appeared in military attire, either as a show of force or because they expected to be met with violence. Stephen Langton acted as the arbiter of the two sides. The outcome of that London meeting was only to postpone the issue until another meeting at the end of April. In the interim, both sides sent appeals to Innocent III, who was technically now John's overlord. John made another calculated gambit. He 'took the cross'; that is, pledged himself to go on a crusade in the Holy Land. This had the effect of endearing him further to Innocent and allowing him to wear the iconic white and red cross. The barons saw his pledge as a sign he was not negotiating in good faith.

On 29 April the two opposing sides met again in Northamptonshire. This time the barons presented the king with a list of demands. John was conciliatory but not inclined to appeasement. He offered some vague compromises—such as a promise to regularly consult a baron's council. But his offer was contingent on papal approval, which, as Innocent was firmly in the royal camp, was not much comfort to the barons. Langton at this stage was still the go-between, but that was itself significant for the progress of the rebellion. A neutral Archbishop of Canterbury was not an Archbishop the king could rely on.

A week later, on 5 May, the barons made their first formal move towards civil war when they renounced the oaths of loyalty to John. This symbolic gesture meant that they no longer considered themselves vassals of the king. Robert Fitzwalter was chosen by the barons as the 'Marshal of the Army of God'. The rebellion was now a military one. The baronial army first marched on Northampton Castle, one of John's possessions, which they were unable to capture. John offered yet more concessions, promising that the demands would be considered by a committee headed by the pope, and that he would not punish any of the rebels except according to the law. Such concessions might have forestalled the rebellion if offered in 1214, but it was too late.

The position of the rebels was strengthened enormously on 17 May when the barons entered London. London was virtually impregnable, too large to besiege, and too important to ignore. The fall of London was a watershed. It caused a 'landslide' of support away from the king. Barons who had been aligned with John switched allegiance to the rebels virtually overnight. John was used to baronial revolts and betrayals on the continent. Now he was experiencing the same in England.

John seems to have recognised how perilous his situation had become. He granted the barons safe travel to London in order to negotiate. The barons gathered at Staines-on-Thames. Stephen Langton also received a letter guaranteeing him safe passage to Staines so that he could arbitrate between the two sides. The chronicler Roger of Wendover, writing almost contemporaneously, gives a simple account of what happened next:

> Accordingly, at the time and place pre-agreed on, the king and nobles came to the appointed conference, and when each party had stationed themselves apart from the other, they began a long discussion about terms of peace and the

aforesaid liberties … At length, after various points on both sides had been discussed, King John, seeing that he was inferior in strength to the barons, without raising any difficulty, granted the underwritten laws and liberties, and confirmed them by his charter.

That place was Runnymede.

Sixty-three Chapters of Liberty

At first sight, the 63 chapters of the Magna Carta follow in no particular order and have no clear method of organisation. Sometimes, related topics are dealt with in entirely different sections of the document, as the sequence of some chapters follows from what was produced in earlier negotiations with the king. Yet presumably at the end the barons were satisfied with the contents of the Magna Carta. Precisely where in the document a promise from the king appeared was less important than that it appeared at all.

The most important chapters in the Magna Carta for the development of liberty are, in order of significance:

- Chapter 39, establishing that punishment can be imposed only after judgement by a person's peers and in accordance with the law,
- Chapter 20, requiring punishment to be proportionate to the gravity of the offence,
- Chapter 40, prohibiting the denial or sale of justice,
- Chapters 12 and 14, requiring the 'common counsel' of the kingdom before the imposition of specific taxes, and
- Chapter 61, on how the Magna Carta was to be enforced.

Chapter 39 is the most famous chapter of the Magna Carta, and its varying translations have already been discussed. The abuse the barons were seeking to overcome was the practice of John to inflict punishments on his opponents without recourse to any legal process. To avoid being inflicted with the arbitrary punishments of the king, his intended victims paid him bribes. As with so much of the Magna Carta, the precise meanings of some of the words in the chapter are unclear. The 'lawful judgement of his peers' did not refer to a trial by a jury—although that is what it was interpreted to mean in later centuries. Rather, 'judgement' referred to the process to determine whether a law had been broken. The meaning of 'law of the land' has proved even more problematic. Most likely it referred to particular legal processes associated with particular offences. But within a few decades it came to signify 'due process of law', and it has been taken to mean that ever since.

Chapter 20 reads:

> A freeman shall not be amerced for a slight offence, except in accordance with the degree of the offence; and for a grave offence he shall be amerced in accordance with the gravity of the offence, yet saving always his contenement; and a merchant in the same way, saving his merchandise, and a villein shall be amerced in the same way, saving his wainage—if they have fallen into our mercy: none of the aforesaid amercements shall be imposed except by the oath of honest men of the neighbourhood.

In simple terms, the chapter means something as basic as that the punishment must fit the crime. For the barons to have demanded such a statement from John reveals the degree to which this principle was disregarded. An 'amercement' was a payment to the crown paid as a penalty after being found guilty of the commission of an offence. Amercements could be paid for offences ranging from failure to attend a meeting of the county to crimes such as robbery.

What precisely a 'freeman' was has long been debated by historians. Perhaps the easiest way to conceive of the term is as someone who was legally free to work and marry as he chose, as opposed to 'villeins', who were bound by law to work on the land of their lord and who could not marry without permission. It is estimated that perhaps half of all peasants were 'free', the other half being 'unfree'.

Why the barons would include a provision protecting villeins is the subject of much argument. The likelihood is that rather than being motivated by any 'humane desire', the barons regarded villeins as akin to their property, and the barons had no desire for the king to destroy the value of their property. The references to freemen not having their 'contenement' confiscated, and likewise the merchandise of merchants and the wainage of villeins, was to ensure that the level of the financial penalties imposed on freemen, merchants, and villeins would not be to such an extent as to make them and their family destitute. In this context 'contenement' referred to a person's means of livelihood, so in other words the chapter ensured that after the payment of an amercement a freeman would still have either enough money or property to sustain themselves. The same principle applied to villeins, as 'wainage' included both a villein's crops and their farming implements.

At first sight, Chapter 40 is the most easily understood of any in the Magna Carta:

> To no one will we sell, to no one will we refuse or delay, right
> or justice.

It reads as an all-embracing promise from the king to ensure justice and judicial impartiality to all people. In reality, the barons were attempting to stop the king from charging exorbitant fees for access to his courts. The king could still impose fees, but they could not be exorbitant.

Hundreds of years later, William McKechnie summed up the great symbolism of Chapter 40:

> … it has been interpreted as a universal guarantee of impartial justice to high and low; and because, when so interpreted, it has become in the hands of patriots in many ages a powerful weapon in the cause of constitutional freedom. Viewing it in this light, [Edward] Coke, [writing in the 1620s] throws aside his crabbed learning and concludes with what is rather a rhapsody than a lawyer's commentary: 'as the gold-finer will not out of the dust, threads, or shreds of gold, let pass the least crumb, in respect of the excellency of the metal; so ought not the learned reader to pass any syllable of this law, in respect of the excellency of the matter.'

Chapter 12 states starkly, 'No scutage or aid is to be imposed on our kingdom, unless by common counsel of our kingdom' and Chapter 14 sets out the process for obtaining that counsel. From these chapters emerged the concept that there should be a measure of consent from taxpayers before tax can be imposed. Notably, the chapter doesn't mention 'consent', for that came later. What the chapters do establish is the right of 'archbishops, bishops, abbots, earls and greater barons' to be consulted about the imposition of two specific taxes—scutage and aid. Centuries later these chapters were transformed into one of the foundations of the British constitutional principle that 'the Crown can impose no financial burden on the people without the consent of Parliament.'

Chapter 61 is the most radical part of the Magna Carta. Here the barons attempted to create an alternative to the authority of king. It is the longest chapter in the Magna Carta and is commonly referred to as the 'Security Clause'. It establishes a council of 25 barons—known as the Twenty-Five—to enforce the terms of the Magna Carta and as 'security' for the good behaviour of John. The Twenty-Five would enforce the terms of the document. If the king or his officials were accused of breaching its terms, the king would be notified and if he didn't rectify the breach, the Twenty-Five were entitled to seize the property of the crown, including the king's castles and lands until 'redress has been obtained'. Furthermore, 'whoever in the country desires it' could take an oath to follow the directions of the Twenty-Five as they enforced the chapter, and anyone who refused to take the oath to the Twenty-Five would be compelled by the king to do so. The chapter was dramatic and draconian for it basically set out the terms on which rebellion was justified. Not surprisingly the chapter was never implemented and was omitted in all subsequent reissues of the Magna Carta. However:

> This chapter has been acclaimed as embodying for the first time the idea that formed 'the true corner stone of the English Constitution,' namely, the right to compel an erring King to bow to a body of law that lies outside his will.

Chapter 61 of course did not detail under what circumstances the kingdom could justifiably rebel against the king. Indeed that question was the starting point for a centuries-long debate about political legitimacy. From this debate came the ideas of political liberalism.

The Magna Carta begins with a preface typical of royal documents of the time. It lists John's advisers, namely, those leading clergy and barons who were still nominally loyal to him, and at the head of the list is Archbishop Stephen Langton. The first chapter contains the king's promise that the English Church is to be free from control of secular authority. It is an uncompromising declaration of the freedom for the English Church:

In the first place we [John] have granted to God, and by this our present charter confirmed for us and our heirs for ever that the English church shall be free, and shall have her rights entire, and her liberties inviolate; and we will that it be thus observed; which is apparent from this that the freedom of elections, which is reckoned most important and very essential to the English church, we, of our pure and unconstrained will, did grant, and did by our charter confirm and did obtain the ratification of the same from our lord, Pope Innocent III, before the quarrel arose between us and our barons: and this we will observe, and our will is that it be observed in good faith by our heirs for ever.

There are no similar provisions in the 49 chapters of the Articles of the Barons. Sometime between the king setting his seal to the Articles and the final drafting of the Magna Carta, it seems that Stephen Langton, the supposedly neutral arbiter between the king and the barons, not only managed to include the church in the Charter, but did so in a way that gave the liberties of the church apparent precedence. The implied purpose of this clause was to separate church and state, and prevent the interference of the latter in the former. The first chapter concludes with the statement that 'We have also granted to all freedmen of our kingdom … all the underwritten liberties'. The effect of these words was to separate the first concession—'granted to God' and the Church—from the remaining concessions, which were addressed to the realm. This resolved the tensions between the privileges of the Church and secular authority firmly in favour of the Church.

After this the Magna Carta deals immediately with the barons' demands, and so Chapters 2 and 3 deal with payments to the king for inheritances, Chapters 4 and 5 with wardships, Chapter 6 with the marriage of heirs, Chapters 7 and 8 with the rights of widows and Chapter 9 with the payment of debts to the king.

Relief, wardship, and payment for marriage were all important sources of revenue for the king, and John had abused all of them. The average payment to the king for consent to marry almost doubled in John's reign, climbing from 174 marks under Richard to a staggering 314 marks. Among many other examples, in 1214 one leader of the baronial faction, John de Lacy, had to pay 7,000 marks in order to inherit his land and be exempted from his father's debt. Another, Geoffrey de Mandeville, was required to pay 20,000 marks to marry Isabella of Gloucester, King John's former wife.

Chapters 10 and 11 dealt with debt to Jews. If someone who had borrowed money from a Jew died, no interest would accrue on the debt while the heir was under age. And if a man died owing a debt, his wife was entitled to claim from the debt her dower and sufficient funds to keep any children 'in a manner in keeping with the holding of the deceased.' These provisions were not only aimed at reducing the debts that the barons owed to the Jews—they were also aimed at the king, because debts owed to Jewish moneylenders could come to be owed to the Crown. Jews were aliens, and the king had practically untrammelled rights over them. 'The Jews themselves and all their possessions are the king's', according to one twelfth century document, *The Laws of Edward the Confessor*. When a Jew died his family had no legal right to the estate— technically it belonged to the Crown. Usually the king claimed one-third of the estate with the rest available to the family. Thus the Magna Carta provisions on Jewish debts were extracted from John himself, since a poorer Jewish population meant less money for the royal treasuries.

After the chapters dealing with money and payments to the king follow a set of six chapters, Chapters 17 to 22, that deal with legal procedures. Chapter 17 grants that royal courts were to be fixed in a certain place.

The first few lines of Chapter 18 are: 'Inquests of *novel disseisin, mort d'ancestor*, and *darrein presentment*, shall not be held elsewhere than in their own county-courts'. This provision requires that court cases about property are to be conducted in the court of the county where the dispute has arisen. This part of the chapter is concerned with the convenience of litigants, who were sometimes forced to travel around the country to have their case heard and incurred significant expense to do so. An 'inquest' was an investigation or a hearing. *Novel disseisin* described what occurred when an individual had been recently dispossessed of land. (*Seisin* was the word for possession, so *disseisin* referred to dispossession and *novel* referred to something that had happened recently.) *Mort d'ancestor* (the 'death of an ancestor') described the right of an heir to claim property possessed by someone else. In medieval England, the right of a lay patron to appoint a cleric to a vacant church position was a form of property. Because the cleric enjoyed the revenues from the position, the right was highly prized, as it could be used to reward a relative or ally, or the right could be sold. The patron 'presented' the candidate for the position to the bishop and so the *darrein presentment* (the 'last presentation') described a dispute as to who had the right to appoint the cleric to a particular position.

Yet even chapters that at first sight have little to do with finance are in fact all about revenue for the king. Chapter 35 declared the units of measurement to be used in the realm for wine, ale, corn, and cloth. For cloth, the unit was to be 'two ells within the selvedge'. An 'ell' was the distance from a man's elbow to the end of his middle finger (deemed to be 45 inches or 1.15 metres) and the 'selvedge' was the edging of the fabric. Cloth could only be sold if it conformed to this standard measure. The chapter had two purposes. The first was to provide convenience to merchants as they moved around the country. The second was to enable the king to levy fines on those who didn't conform to the standard measure.

Chapter 26 governed how debts were to be resolved from the estate of a crown tenant upon their death. Sheriffs had the habit of seizing all available property, regardless of what was owed, and the Magna Carta required the lawful accounting of debts in front of neighbours as a check on such expropriation. Chapter 35 allocated who was to receive the property of people who had been convicted of felonies: John had claimed ownership over all property owned by felons, but under Magna Carta that property was to revert within a year to the felon's feudal lord.

Other chapters established the scope of liberties already asserted. For instance, the right to travel outside England's borders was given a firm footing in Chapter 42, which allowed any person, except prisoners, exiles, and foreign enemies, to 'leave our kingdom and to return, safe and secure by land and water … reserving always the allegiance due to us.' John had reserved permission to travel for himself. Chapter 42 established a fundamental freedom of movement. The access of merchants to England was governed by Chapter 41, which not only allowed their 'safe and secure exit from England, and entre to England' but protected them from the 'evil tolls' that John had imposed in his desperate revenue raising.

On top of restraints on the king's expropriation, the Magna Carta offers a miscellany of legal reforms and administrative changes. Some chapters resolved diplomatic issues in the context of a nascent civil war. Oppressive exactions imposed on Wales were rectified by Chapters 56 and 57. Welsh hostages were released by Chapter 58. Scottish relations were re-established by Chapter 59. Others protected the interests of the church—such as Chapter 46, which secured the rights of barons who had founded abbeys from being usurped by the king. Further chapters regulated John's control of the royal forest. But despite the apparent diversity of the Magna Carta's provisions, almost every chapter had one goal in mind: to rebalance political and economic power away from the king and towards the barons and a Church independent from the king.

The Magna Carta was extracted out of a weak and humiliated king, and the barons took advantage of his diminished power to right previous wrongs and lock in future victories. Chapter 52 granted that assets—'castles, liberties, or rights'—taken without lawful judgement were to be restored. Likewise, Chapter 53 granted that 'all fines that have been given to us unjustly and against the law of the land, and all fines that we have exacted unjustly should be remitted or judged through a set process.' The last chapter of the Magna Carta, Chapter 63, would allow future generations to read into the document practically any conceivable freedom:

> Wherefore we wish and firmly command that the English Church will be free, and the men in our realm will have and hold all the aforesaid liberties, rights and concessions well and peacefully, freely and quietly, fully and completely for themselves and their heirs of us and our heirs in all things and places for ever, as is aforesaid.

CHAPTER SEVEN

FROM PEACE TREATY TO CONSTITUTION

The Magna Carta did not secure peace. The fault was not John's alone. While perhaps negotiations were made at Runnymede in goodwill, the subsequent events demonstrated that neither the barons nor the monarch saw the Magna Carta as anything approaching a resolution of the conflict. Yet by the end of the thirteenth century, the Magna Carta became an icon against the arbitrary rule of monarchs.

There were a number of reasons why the Magna Carta failed to stop the war between King John and the barons. Many of its chapters were vague. For all the document's implicit reference to reasonableness, there was no guiding principle by which debates at the margin could be resolved. The Twenty-Five was a mechanism to keep the king in check not by law but by force. Some barons had greater ambitions for the Magna Carta than could strictly be read into the document. For some, the position of the Twenty-Five was not simply as an enforcement mechanism but an alternative source of political power to the crown—a sort of shadow government with its own authority. The Magna Carta provides for the king to be ruled by law, not by barons. Some of the Twenty-Five apparently felt otherwise, believing that the king had to pay homage to them. On a purely practical level, the most obvious evidence that contemporaries could see for the Magna Carta's failure was the fact that the rebels neither disarmed nor relinquished London. Robert Fitzwalter even kept up his title as Marshal of the Army of God. England remained on the brink of civil war.

John, for his part, had little interest in upholding the charter. For him, it was a treaty whose only value was to keep him on the throne. John's ambivalence was clear from the first moment it was sealed. A peace treaty need only be understood by those who are a party to the treaty. By contrast, a tax constitution needed to be distributed to those who paid the taxes and those who collected the taxes. John made it as difficult as possible for copies of the document to be distributed. But, in a win for the barons, the charter was distributed nonetheless.

The process of John restoring the lands confiscated from the rebel barons, as required by the Magna Carta, began immediately. John acquiesced quickly to most claims and tried to delay others, but for the most part restoration happened rapidly, regardless of the king's reticence. Castles were returned to their former owners. Eustace de Vesci, for his part, had his right to run his dogs in the forest of Northumberland restored.

Within weeks of Runnymede, it was clear peace could not be

sustained. In early July, letters arrived from Innocent III—who was yet unaware of the meeting at Runnymede—excommunicating the barons opposed to John. John dispatched an appeal to the pope claiming he had been coerced into accepting the terms of the charter. The pope was happy to help his vassal. Probably by the end of September, the news had come from Rome that Innocent had annulled the Magna Carta. It was, as the papal edict said, 'to the detriment of the royal right and the shame of the English nation'. The Magna Carta was inspired by Satan, 'shameful and demeaning ... illegal and unjust'. With the pope's blessing, John repudiated the charter.

The result was war. John was prepared. He had been carefully building up his resources after Runnymede, expecting the conflict to escalate. Sometime either at the end of August or the beginning of September, the rebels met and decided to replace John and offer the English crown to Prince Louis, the eldest son of King Philip Augustus of France. Louis had a tenuous claim on the English throne through his marriage to Blanche of Castile, a granddaughter of King Henry II.

A French army invaded England in May 1216. In June they entered London. Louis was proclaimed king. Many barons—including some very close to John—paid homage to Louis. Yet fighting between John's forces on one side and the rebel barons and the French on the other continued throughout 1216. French forces laid siege to Dover, Lincoln, and Windsor, while the Scots threatened royal castles in the north. In September, John defeated the rebels' siege of his castle at Lincoln and then turned south to face the French. John had some successes, and some barons who had handed their allegiance to Louis and the rebels had drifted back to the king over the course of the year. Yet John's days were numbered. At Lynn in Norfolk, John became ill with dysentery.

On 12 October, while the king's baggage train was crossing the sand flats on the border of Norfolk and Lincolnshire known as the Wash, the tide came in before the crossing could be completed. The royal treasure, including the king's crown, was lost in the sea and sand. Six days later John died at Newark Castle, aged 49.

John's last act was to try to arrange his succession. The king's eldest son was Henry, who was just nine years old. John appointed as regent one of his loyal supporters, the battle-hardened William Marshal, Earl of Pembroke. Marshal's first move was to have Henry crowned as soon as possible, with the coronation occurring at Gloucester Cathedral nine days after John's death.

Henry III ruled over a country in disarray, with the royal government seriously considering withdrawal to Ireland. Marshal promised never to desert the boy 'even if I have to beg my bread', and carry Henry 'from island to island and from land to land'. The royalist cause was helped by the fact that Louis and the rebels were unable to obtain papal approval to crown Louis in England. Over the next few months, more barons moved back to the royal camp, especially when Louis returned to the continent searching for reinforcements. In two major battles in May and August 1217, Marshal's forces defeated Louis and the rebels, first in a brutal battle within the walls of the city of Lincoln, and then in a naval clash off the coast of Sandwich. Louis sued for peace and subsequently agreed to the Treaty of Lambeth in September 1217. He agreed to leave England and relinquish his claim to the English throne. In return he was paid 10,000 marks—equal to a quarter of the Crown's annual income.

In November 1216, Marshal had made the momentous decision to reissue the Magna Carta as an attempt to placate the rebel barons. Some changes were made to the document on its reissue (for instance, the guarantee of free Church elections was removed), but in essence it remained the same. At the first instance, this ploy did not succeed. So much blood had been spilled between the rebels and royalists that no document would hold back the fighting. Yet the rebels didn't have the same animosity towards the nine-year-old Henry as they did to his father. Already in 1216 the Magna Carta was becoming less a specific peace treaty in the context of the politics of June 1215, and more a general outline of liberties to which future kings would have to adhere.

Despite the treaty with Louis and the cessation of outright hostilities, Henry's control of England was far from absolute. The barons had been empowered by the rebellion, refusing feudal dues at times and resisting royal authority when it suited. It took a decade for the Angevin administrative supremacy enjoyed by Richard to be re-established and for the rule of Henry to be normalised.

In a further effort to establish its rule, the government of Henry reissued the Magna Carta again in November 1217. It differed from the earlier issues because it separated into a separate charter the provisions dealing with the administration of the royal forests. In 1217, therefore, Henry assented to both the Magna Carta and the new Forest Charter. While John tried to limit the distribution of his 1215 charter, Henry's government wished to spread knowledge of the new charter far and wide. In February 1218, under the guidance of Marshal, Henry ordered that the two charters be observed throughout the realm.

William Marshal died in 1219. In the wake of his death, the now thirteen-year-old Henry was re-crowned king with all new regalia and the pope's blessing. Henry, it seemed, now had nearly all the barons on side. Even those who had gone to war with the French against him now stood in homage at his re-coronation.

Yet even as he established tighter control, he was reaffirming his allegiance to the charter. At a great council in 1223, Henry reconfirmed the Magna Carta.

In 1224, Louis, now reigning in France as King Louis VIII, invaded what was left of Angevin possessions in France. Henry, like his father, was not about to let his European possessions fade into memory. The mayor of Bordeaux wrote to the English king deferentially: 'If it pleases you to send us help in both men and money, you will recover your lands'. But Henry had no money. Furthermore, France had long ago outpaced England in the race for financial dominance. Louis considered Henry 'a boy and a pauper'. Despite his growing authority at home, Henry's revenue base was hardly secure. The Magna Carta of 1215 appeared to have definitively abolished the king's power to levy scutage without the common consent of the realm. The 1217 edition of the charter insisted that the only just scutage allowed to be levied was that 'as it was accompanied in the time of Henry our Grandfather'. A scutage levied in 1217 was a failure, raising just a few thousand pounds. A land tax levied in 1220 was likewise disappointing. Henry might have been king, but baronial fealty was not so great as to preclude widespread tax evasion.

In February 1225, Henry assembled a great council in London to consider the situation on the continent. The lack of baronial interest in France had not changed since John's time: few barons had any financial interests on the continent and were not particularly inspired to defend Henry's inheritance. Nevertheless, they were moved by the potential threat that Louis posed. Louis had staked a claim to England before and might do so again. The council approved a relief force to Gascony, led by the king's sixteen-year-old brother, Richard, accompanied by William Longespée. But paying for this military adventure would require a new, and substantial, tax on England. Henry offered to renew the Magna Carta and the Forest Charter in exchange for a substantial tax—one-fifteenth of the value of moveables.

This was a watershed moment in English history. The last tax on moveables had been imposed in 1207, and had helped plunge England into civil war. By offering to renew the Magna Carta and the Forest Charter in exchange for permission to levy another tax, Henry formalised the Magna Carta into the English constitution.

The 1225 version of the Magna Carta was the final iteration of the document. Although it would be reissued later in the century under Edward I, its terms would not be rewritten. There were some substantial differences between the 1215 Magna Carta and that of 1225. The 1225 charter contains only 37 chapters according to most modern editions. The 1215 Magna Carta was divided by Blackstone in the eighteenth century, while the chapters of the 1225 edition were devised following a sixteenth century edition of the document. Therefore, many sections that appear as separate chapters in the 1215 document (for example, Chapters 39 and 40) are combined into a single chapter in most modern editions of the 1225 charter (in this case, Chapter 29). In addition, four entirely new chapters appeared in the 1225 charter. There were restrictions on the disposal of land and limits on gifts of property to religious houses, county courts were prevented from being held more than once a month, and scutage could only be levied on the terms it had been levied under during the reign of Henry II.

There were two stark absences. The 'security' chapter was missing. Henry III was not about to hand over political power to a council of barons. And the all-important scutage chapter (Chapter 14 in the 1215 Magna Carta), which set out the process through which the king could obtain the 'common counsel' of the realm for scutage and aids, was removed. The 1225 version of the Magna Carta lacked the institutional checks that had been imposed on John. In part this is because the 1225 Magna Carta was issued in entirely different circumstances.

There was no civil war and no suggestion the king had been coerced. Indeed, the 1225 text emphasised that Henry III had given the whole charter voluntarily:

> Know that we, out of reverence for God and for the salvation of our soul and the souls of our ancestors and successors, for the exaltation of holy church and the reform of our realm, *have of our own spontaneous goodwill given and granted* to the archbishops, bishops, abbots, priors, earls, barons and all of our realm these liberties written below to be held in our kingdom of England for ever … [emphasis added]

The closing chapter of the 1225 charter includes a lengthy list of witnesses, including some who had supported the rebel cause in 1215 like Robert Fitzwalter. And the 1225 Magna Carta made explicit that the king was reconfirming certain rights in exchange for permission to impose a tax:

> In return for this grant and gift of these liberties and of the other liberties contained in our charter on the liberties of the forest, the archbishops, bishops, abbots, priors, earls, barons, knights, freeholders and all of our realm have given us a fifteenth part of all their movables.

The seeking of permission to levy taxation had evolved into a constitutional norm. Any future attempts to levy taxes without the counsel of the realm would be vigorously opposed. And the Church supported the document as well. Any person who violated the charter was threatened with excommunication.

The 1225 Magna Carta, like the 1215 document before it, was a quintessentially English document sealed by a king whose eyes were firmly on Europe. Henry III had wished to defend, and in his more ambitious moments, restore, the great empire of his grandfather. The tax on moveables was highly successful. But the military campaign it financed was not. When a peace treaty was signed with King Louis IX of France (Louis VIII had died in 1226), the territorial situation was basically as it had been in 1225.

John had been forced by civil war to trade his royal prerogative for revenue. Henry III gave his prerogatives up freely, if not totally happily. Father and son believed they were pursuing a greater goal by doing so: the restoration of the lands of Henry II. Henry was an Angevin king, and Angevin kings were European kings, not English ones. To the Angevins, England was little more than a regional outpost that the dynasty had temporarily retreated to, most useful for its financial resources. John had learned that not all English barons were as focussed on continental Europe as he was. The northerners had closer relationships with Scotland than Normandy, and Aquitaine and Poitou were far from England. The failure to rebuild the Angevin empire dramatically changed the long-term direction of government in England.

Henry III's conciliatory approach, which had so successfully tamed a country coming out of civil war, did not last. He began his personal rule—that is, rule in his own right rather than through a regent on his behalf—in 1234. After almost two decades of being overshadowed by his father's ministers, Henry began to exhibit some of the characteristics he had inherited from his lineage. In Poitou the French suppressed a revolt against their rule instigated by supporters of the English king. Henry fruitlessly led an army to the continent, but failed to retake the region. With the French stamping their authority on Poitou, Henry invited loyal Poitevins to England, granting them lands and titles. Henry had married a Poitevin, Eleanor of Provence, and his new relations began to populate the English administrative apparatus. The same anti-French sentiment which had met the father's royal appointments was visited on his son's.

Henry unsurprisingly kept his European ambitions burning. He tried to rebuild alliances in the lost territories. He tried, and failed, to place his younger son Edmund on the throne of Sicily. These ambitions cost money. After 1225, the great council approved a series of taxes to finance his efforts in France. Yet the council's support was not absolute, as one meeting of the council demonstrated in March 1232, when they refused Henry's justiciar, Hubert de Burgh, a tax to pay for the debts resulting from a failed campaign in Wales. For a short time, Henry tried to resist the strictures of the Magna Carta, but the response was resistance and a revolt under Richard Marshal—the son of William Marshal.

The word 'parliament' first appears in English records in 1236 to describe the great councils at which Henry III appealed for money. He went to parliament again in 1237 to ask for money to pay for the dowry of his sister, Isabella, who had been married to the German Emperor Frederick. In an acrimonious meeting where grievances over his past conduct, fiscal recklessness, and revenue raising were aired, Henry was forced to reaffirm the Magna Carta. Parliament's control of the purse strings of government gave it scope to consider a wider breadth of government activity. Parliaments became occasions to hear legal cases and conduct royal ceremony.

Parliament of the early reign of Henry III was not the institution as we know it today. It was not formed by election or according to any principles of representation. Yet the Magna Carta had formally established a relationship between tax and consent that provided legitimacy for revenue raising. Under Henry, the assembly of parliament was not restricted only to barons and the upper clergy but began to take in some knights, lesser landholders, and the lower clergy. Even with this slight expansion, parliament adopted the fiction that the realm was 'represented' in some way by the upper and upper-middle nobility. Such a concept of representation did not last for more than a few decades. If Henry wanted to tax the whole community he would have to gain the consent of the community. In 1254 the king summoned a parliament comprising of both the magnates and two knights from each shire who could speak on their shires' behalf.

One of the nobles who Henry attracted to England from France was Simon de Montfort. Born around 1208, he was the son of a French-English noble. When he came to England in 1229 de Montfort ingratiated himself with the king. His relationship with Henry was so close that he was made a godfather to the king's son, Edward. De Montfort also married the king's sister, Eleanor.

Henry III had a precarious hold on what remained of the English crown's French possessions because of the constant risk of rebellion in Gascony. Henry convinced de Montfort to take up the position of viceroy. After taking the role in 1248, de Montfort was accused by the Gascons of oppressive administration. Henry took up the cause of his dissatisfied continental subjects and put de Montfort on trial in 1252. This was an acrimonious event. Henry levelled charges of cruelty at de Montfort. In return de Montfort accused Henry of having ignored the terms under which he had accepted the post and the king's previous instructions to suppress rebellion. At one stage de Montfort accused his king of 'unchristian' behaviour. But de Montfort had the almost unanimous support of the English magnates in parliament. The trial was suspended in June 1252. All this drama placed de Montfort squarely in the anti-Henry camp throughout the 1250s. He was among those barons who led parliamentary efforts to deny Henry taxes throughout that decade, positioning himself as a leader when the crisis began in 1258.

In April 1258, Henry held a parliament to raise a new round of taxes to finance his foreign policy. Henry made an unprecedented request—he sought approval for a tax of one-third of the value and income on all moveables *and* immoveables, principally land. This would have been the largest single tax ever levied by an Angevin king, both in its scale and breadth. Richard's ransom six decades earlier had only been levied on moveables. Unsurprisingly, the parliament's response was hostile. The barons, now led by de Montfort, took the opportunity to extract concessions from the king. Rather than trading their consent to the tax for reconfirmation of the Magna Carta, they insisted on a broader reform movement. And they only offered to consider the new tax at a new reform parliament.

Later that year, the resulting Oxford parliament, also known as the 'mad' parliament, sought to enhance and solidify parliament's constitutional role. De Montfort and the barons put forward the 'Provisions of Oxford'. The Provisions were informed by the decades of experience of trying to enforce the principles of the Magna Carta on an unwilling and rapacious king. Rather than detailed rules about specific taxes and rules of inheritance, the 1258 document focuses on the institutional setting of Parliament. It provided for the establishment of a fifteen-person baronial council with the power to appoint the king's ministers. This council would be overseen by Parliament, whose meetings were for the first time scheduled to occur three times a year. While Henry remained at the head of the government as king, the council of fifteen and the king formed the executive arm of government, in charge of day-to-day issues. Parliament, for its part, was given a legislative role, with the barons again using the king's need for tax approval to expand its jurisdiction into many other areas of political responsibility.

The echoes of the Magna Carta in the Provisions of Oxford

are obvious, and de Montfort and the barons said they were en-
acting and enforcing the principles which had been established
at Runnymede. For the many chapters in the Magna Carta, the
pivot on which political power rested was a few words—'by the
common counsel'—and the unworkable security clause. Under
Henry III those institutional hints took on a life of their own,
formalising into rules which divided power between kings and
barons. The Provisions of Oxford were revised and finalised in the
Provisions of Westminster in 1259.

The parliamentary reforms of 1258-59 were repudiated by
Henry in 1261, and the decision propelled de Montfort into outright rebellion. The result was what is now known as the Second
Baronial War, the First Baronial War being that fought against
John. De Montfort headed the discontented baronial faction. In
1264, at the Battle of Lewes, de Montfort's forces captured Henry
and his son Edward.

De Montfort effectively ruled England in his own right. He
continued the project of parliamentary reform. Aware of the need
to maintain broad political support, he summoned representatives
from the shires to attend his parliaments. He had himself at-
tended Henry's parliament of 1254, to which shire representatives
had been invited for the first time. Two parliaments met in June
1264 and January 1265 that included elected representatives of
the shires, and in the latter case, of the towns. It is his rebellion
against Henry and his leadership of the Second Baronial War
that is popularly credited with the invention of parliament and
the introduction of commoners into the English political settlement. In fact, de Montfort followed the developing tradition of
parliamentary government. Henry III, not de Montfort, invited
the first representatives of the shires to a 'parliament'. It is to this
that the House of Commons can trace its origins.

De Montfort's rule did not last long. In a battle at Evesham in August 1265, de Montfort was defeated and killed by Henry's son Edward, who would later rule as Edward I. Henry III resumed the throne.

Nevertheless, de Montfort's rebellion is the constitutional bookend to the troubles of the thirteenth century, a crisis of English government that enshrined a division between parliament and the king that would endure for centuries.

Throughout all these disturbances, the Magna Carta remained unscathed. In 1267 and 1270 Henry reaffirmed the document. The Magna Carta had value for the monarchy as well. Henry—and later his formidable son Edward—were able to claim that the barons had exceeded the authority delineated at Runnymede. Edward reissued the Magna Carta again in 1297. It was now entrenched in the English constitution.

EIGHT

MAGNA CARTA AND ENGLISH LIBERTIES

Political power is ultimately maintained by a combination of custom, expectations of behaviour, force, and the threat of force. The United Kingdom is often described as unusual because its constitution is 'unwritten'. But all constitutions are at least partly unwritten, resting key features of governance on tradition, precedent, and long-standing practice. While the 1225 Magna Carta did not contain anything requiring the consent of magnates to tax, by the time of Henry III, the expectation that the king would need to gain some form of consent before a tax could be imposed was part of England's constitution.

In the medieval era, parliament's authority came to rest ultimately on its control over the purse strings of government.

All of parliament's legislative authority derived from the implied threat that its members could withhold money from the Crown. When parliament scrutinised the actions of the king, or approved his wishes, it could do so only because of its power over taxation. In many ways the relationship between the Crown and parliament in the sixteenth and seventeenth centuries was not unlike that between the Angevin kings and their barons. Elizabeth I, James I, and Charles I could, to some extent, draw upon their own sources of revenue, particularly from Crown lands, to sustain the operations of government. But whenever there was a requirement for additional finances gained from taxes, the monarch had to resort to parliament. In the 1600s the question of precisely which financial exactions levied by the crown required parliamentary approval would be one of the causes of the English Civil War.

If a constitution as the basis for a system of government administration is to rely on norms of behaviour, it is important that both rulers and the ruled share those norms. Neither James I nor his son Charles I shared those norms. They both believed they had a religiously ordained right to rule. In 1609 James declared to parliament, 'The State of Monarchie is the supremest thing upon earth: For Kings are not onely Gods Lieutenants upon earth, and sit upon Gods throne, but even by God himselfe they are called Gods.' The crown's enthusiasm for royal absolutism was due in part to the Reformation. Prior to the break with Rome the head of the church in England had been the Pope, and the head of secular government was the king. But after the 1534 *Act of Supremacy* of Henry VIII, which declared that the English king was the supreme head of the Church of England, spiritual and temporal power came to be united in the English crown.

The doctrine of 'divine right' was unlikely to impress parliament. James I had claimed that 'as to dispute what God may do is blasphemy, so it is sedition in subjects to dispute what a King may do in the height of his power.' Parliament was *his* agency: it derived its legitimacy from the king's person, not from any other principle of representation or the common counsel. If there was an intellectual shift in the way James I and Charles I saw themselves, there was a corresponding shift in the way parliament saw itself. Parliament responded vigorously to his claims for godly authority:

> We hold it an ancient, general, and undoubted right of Parliament to debate freely all matters which properly concern the subject and his right or state; which freedom of debate being once foreclosed, the essence of the liberty of Parliament is withal dissolved.

James' relationship with parliament was acrimonious, and when he dismissed the parliament in 1611 it was only to meet briefly in 1614 before being finally recalled in 1621. James wanted to rule without parliament but his government's expenditure was large. He spent more in peacetime than Elizabeth had spent while at war. His extravagance was evident from the moment he ascended to the English throne.

Yet for all his claims of divine authority, James could not sidestep the fundamental constitutional compact which required parliament's approval for taxes. James had dissolved the 1614 parliament when it would not pass any financial legislation. For the next seven years, James attempted to govern in his own right, finding funds in as many creative ways as possible. This included a forced loan in 1614, the sale of two small Dutch towns possessed by the English crown, and a loan from the city of London.

James was compelled to summon another parliament in 1621 when his revenue needs became acute. This meeting began well, but floundered on parliament's insistence that it could debate the king's foreign policy. Parliament proclaimed 'the liberties, franchises, privileges and jurisdictions of parliament are the ancient and undoubted birthright and inheritance of the subjects of England' and that the body had every right to debate and discuss anything concerning 'the king, state and defence of the realm'. James' response was to dissolve the parliament once more.

The principal author of that proclamation was Sir Edward Coke, one of the most remarkable and significant figures in English parliamentary history. Coke was a parliamentary elder, a major political and intellectual force, and had been the monarch's most important legal adviser. Born in 1552, he trained as a barrister, and became a member of parliament in 1588. He thrived under Elizabeth I and then under James I, prosecuting for treason such notables as Sir Walter Raleigh and the eight surviving conspirators of the Gunpowder Plot, including Guy Fawkes. Coke gained numerous senior judicial appointments.

On the surface, Coke's career looks a picture of loyalty to the monarch, but he was in fact one of the great theorists of the 'ancient constitution', which bound and restrained the prerogative of the monarch. For Coke, England was governed by a common law whose heritage stretched back to before the Norman Conquest. In his view the Magna Carta affirmed the laws and the liberties as they had always existed in England—it was the 'roote' from which 'many fruitfull branches of the Law of England have sprung'.

Coke's interpretations of key provisions of the Magna Carta stretched beyond the plausible. More than anybody else, he inculcated the idea that the thirteenth century document laid a detailed foundation of English liberties. In his hands, the requirement that scutages and aids be approved by the common counsel of the realm became parliament's right to approve taxation. Thirteenth century notions of feudal custom became allegiance to the common law. Parliament itself became an ancient institution that no king could abridge, with authority drawn from pre-Conquest England, rather than the ad hoc and contingent institutional development of reality. Indeed, he even argued that the 1225 Magna Carta had been legitimised by a sitting of parliament.

Coke was an intensely political man and his interpretations were tailored to the concerns of the seventeenth century. A contemporary critic of Coke wrote:

> It is to be observed throughout all his books that he hath as it were purposely laboured to derogate much from the rights of the church and dignity of churchmen; to disesteem and weaken the power of the king in the ancient use of his prerogatives; to traduce or else to cut short the jurisdiction of all other courts besides that court wherein himself doth sit.

Such antipathy towards the royal prerogative unsurprisingly put Coke at loggerheads with James I. Coke was dismissed as a judge in 1616. He quickly became one of the leading opposition parliamentarians, challenging James' demands for revenue.

Coke did not invent the intellectual connection between the Magna Carta and ideas of English liberty. They were, indeed, in nascent form at Runnymede as 'ancient liberties', and the 'rights' of London and the Church. But Coke transformed the Magna Carta from a detailed peace treaty speaking to specific concerns of the barons in 1215 to become a fundamental statement of the English constitutional compact.

James I died in March 1625 and his son Charles ascended to the throne as Charles I. The marriage in May 1625 of Charles to a Catholic wife, Henrietta Maria, a daughter of Henry IV of France, inflamed parliament. Also problematic was that the new king had a more bellicose foreign policy than his father.

Charles agitated for war against Spain, a country with which England had last been at war under Elizabeth. In April, Charles had summoned a parliament to gain its permission to levy 'tonnage and poundage' (customs duties) for his lifetime. The parliament refused, giving him permission to impose duties for only one year. The king was granted limited funds for a naval raid against Spain.

The Spanish venture was a disaster. A joint British-Dutch expedition failed to capture the well-fortified city of Cadiz, failed to intercept a fleet of Spanish galleons, and returned to England in defeat. The campaign permanently soured Charles' relations with parliament.

His war with Spain continued but parliament was more interested in fighting him than fighting another country. In 1626 the king dissolved parliament and attempted to get around it by levying a forced loan. In truth the loan was a tax, because nobody expected that those forced to lend money to the government would ever see those funds again. When a group of landowners (the 'Five Knights') refused to make the loan, they were imprisoned. The dispute ended in a court case which the king won on the basis that he had the legal authority to levy the loan, but the controversy caused him lasting political damage. The imprisoned men were finally released in 1628.

In 1629 Charles dissolved parliament and tried to rule without it. He concluded peace with Spain, reduced expenditure as much as he could, relied on feudal and non-parliamentary levies, and used compliant courts to push the boundaries of what was legal. Charles' behaviour over this period prompted parliament to produce the famous and important Petition of Right. In May 1628 the Petition was presented to the king as a declaration from parliament. It was drafted by a group of parliamentarians including Edward Coke to be a reaffirmation of what were regarded as the principles of the Magna Carta. It declared no man 'should be put out of his land or tenements, nor taken, nor imprisoned, nor disinherited nor put to death without being brought to answer by due process of law.' Furthermore, 'no man hereafter be compelled to make or yield any gift, loan, benevolence, tax, or such like charge, without common consent by act of parliament'. The echoes of the Magna Carta—'The Great Charter of the Liberties of England'—were deliberate. Coke and his colleagues believed that they were simply re-establishing the ancient rights of parliament against a king desperate to usurp them.

Charles had been willing to reissue the Magna Carta. He was reluctant, however, to endorse a new charter that extended and expanded the liberties of parliament. Nevertheless, facing serious financial needs in wartime, he accepted the Petition of Right. In the nineteenth century, historian Lord Macaulay wrote:

> The day on which the royal sanction was, after many delays, solemnly given to this great Act, was a day of joy and hope. The Commons, who crowded the bar of the House of Lords, broke forth into loud acclamations as soon as the clerk had pronounced the ancient form of words by which our princes have, during many ages, signified their assent to the wishes of the Estates of the realm. Those acclamations were reechoed by the voice of the capital and of the nation.

Yet this joy was fleeting. By the time the 1629 parliament was dissolved, Charles had repudiated the principles of the Petition of Right. Like its ancestor the Magna Carta, the Petition of Right was initially a failure, unable to prevent the breakdown of the relationship between the king and his magnates.

For the decade he ruled without parliament, Charles had two major sources of revenue. The first was the sale of monopolies. Since Henry VIII, the crown had been handing out monopoly rights and licences as favours for service or directly for money. Royal government was cash poor but had powers for which people were willing to pay handsomely. Under Charles, the sale of these monopolies increased exponentially. Monopolies could be granted on the import of goods, the manufacture and sale of goods, and even the enforcement of prohibitions on goods. In many ways, this was an extension of the feudal system for a commercial age. In the thirteenth century land and labour were the great economic assets. But by the seventeenth century the economy was much more complex, with more diverse sources of wealth. The king believed those sources were his to control and dispense. Charles' monopolies were much resented by parliament. Indeed, the 1624 parliament had passed a law—the *Statute of Monopolies*, today recognised as the foundational source of modern intellectual property law—restraining Charles' monopoly making. Nevertheless, Charles defiantly expanded his monopoly granting while parliament wasn't sitting.

Charles' second major source of revenue was 'Ship Money'. This tax had medieval origins. Feudal kings could compel maritime towns and counties to provide ships in time of war. Just as scutage had been levied in place of knights' service, kings would often accept money in place of physical ships. This was a rarely used power, to the extent that it meant it was unclear as to whether it required parliamentary approval to levy. Shortly before her death in 1603, Elizabeth, concerned about Spanish attacks on English shipping, had extended the principle of Ship Money to cover not only jurisdictions beside the sea, but the whole country. Charles first tried to levy Ship Money in 1628, almost immediately after having confirmed the Petition of Right, and without parliament's approval. The attempt was quickly withdrawn.

A more consequential levying of Ship Money began in 1634. Rather than a one-off tax, Charles decided to levy Ship Money nationally and annually, making it a permanent national tax.

Ship Money was deeply unpopular and deeply resented, on par with the resentment met by the forced loan of 1629. Those liable to pay resisted, both because of the financial burden and because it was seen as an illegitimate tax. When it was first nationally levied in 1634, the measure was relatively successful, but returns from Ship Money declined starkly in subsequent years and took longer to collect.

Ship Money and the sale of monopolies had sustained Charles' expenditure for a decade. But by 1640, declining revenue came up against a new demand for spending. Charles wanted to send an army to Scotland but lacked the funds to do so. He unhappily recalled parliament for funds. This 'Short Parliament' lasted less than a month, between mid-April and early May 1640. Parliament had not sat for ten years and it took the opportunity to redress grievances that had built up over a decade. Charles dismissed the parliament in frustration. He launched a military campaign against Scotland without parliament's fiscal or political support. The campaign was disastrous. Within a few months, it resulted in a Scottish army occupying Newcastle, demanding £850 a day for a guarantee not to launch further incursions into England, and bribes to return home. A humiliated Charles once again recalled parliament to seek funds.

The 'Long Parliament' was summoned in November 1640 and was not dissolved until 1648. Charles wanted parliament to approve new revenue, but it was more interested in imposing its control over the monarch. Parliament impeached Charles' associates—the Archbishop of Canterbury and Charles' closest advisor Thomas Wentworth, the Earl of Stafford. The archbishop was imprisoned in February 1641. Charles reluctantly signed the death warrant for Stafford in May the same year. Parliament also went about imposing institutional changes on the formation and dissolution of parliament. The *Triennial Acts*, passed in February 1641 with the king's consent, required parliament to meet for at least fifty days once every three years. They prohibited the dissolution of parliament without the consent of parliament itself. The personal rule of the king was to end. The Long Parliament also prohibited the raising of funds without parliament's consent, the imposition of Ship Money, and the levying of forced loans.

The Long Parliament was revolutionary. It was literally 'revolutionary' because the members of the Long Parliament helped make up the parliamentary army that would go to war against the king. Its legislative program was also revolutionary. The *Triennial Acts* established parliament as an authority independent of the crown—as a body not relying for its existence on the goodwill of the monarch. When parliament asserted itself it did so under the belief that it was merely adhering to the ancient tradition symbolised—if not created—by the Magna Carta itself. Edward Coke had died in 1634, but his arguments formed the basis of political rhetoric throughout the period. One parliamentarian summarised how parliament regarded its role:

> The Charter of our Liberties, called Magna Carta ... was but a renovation and restitution of the ancient laws of this kingdom ... and in the third year of [Charles I], we had more than a conformation of it; for we had an act declaratory passed, and then, to put it out of all question and dispute for the future, his Majesty ... invested it with the title of Petition of Right. What expositions contrary to that law of right have

some men given to the underestimating the liberty of the subject with new-invented subtle distinctions, and assuming to themselves a power … out of Parliament to supersede, annihilate and make void the laws of the kingdom?

An iconic act of the first months of the Long Parliament was the *Habeas Corpus Act* of 1640. Revised in 1679, the *Habeas Corpus Act* remains substantially part of English law today. To understand how deeply the Magna Carta was tied to the English political compact, it is worth looking at how Chapter 39 of the 1215 Magna Carta was transformed into *habeas corpus*.

The origins of *habeas corpus*—a Latin phrase literally translated as 'you should have the body'—can be traced back to the legal reforms of Henry II. Coke and his contemporaries identified the Magna Carta as the source of the idea that a person could only be imprisoned by the judgement of his peers and by the law of the land. In fact this reading of the Magna Carta was quite wrong. The Magna Carta had been written in a time when King John would take hostages from a baron's family to ensure their loyalty or as security for the payment of taxes. The concept of 'arrest' for a crime was embryonic in the thirteenth century. The relationship between *habeas corpus* and basic legal rights like trial by jury, trial under law and due process, is by no means linear or self-evident. Yet the relationship mattered for seventeenth century politics. When Charles imprisoned the Five Knights for refusing to pay the forced loan of 1627, he violated the Magna Carta. Charles had used arbitrary imprisonment as a punishment for tax evasion. The establishment of a statutory common law right to *habeas corpus* comes from parliament's resentment over the coercive nature of the monarch's revenue raising system.

The furore over *habeas corpus* under Charles is another illustration of how disputes over taxation have spiralled into broader concerns about political power. Tax is the state's most fundamental power—both necessary for the functioning of the state and, particularly in the medieval and early modern period, the locus of most individuals' interaction with the state. Imposing a hated tax on an unwilling population necessitates broad coercive measures. Charles, like John four hundred years earlier, learned that aggressive revenue raising equated to oppression. By the time of the Long Parliament, Charles' parliamentary opponents felt in command enough to pursue a broader reform agenda that touched on matters well beyond just the control of taxation. If there had been a royal alternative to Charles it is possible the conflict would not have escalated the way that it did. As it was, rule by parliament was the only alternative to rule by Charles. Half a century later there *was* an alternative to James II, another unpopular king. Thus in the 'Glorious' Revolution of 1688, parliament invited William of Orange to become king of England, replacing James II.

After two years of attempting to deal with a belligerent parliament, Charles made a fateful decision. In January 1642, he marched into parliament, backed by armed soldiers, to arrest five MPs he believed had encouraged the Scots to invade England. However those five—who included one of Charles' leading critics, John Pym—had already fled. Worried for his safety, Charles left London.

It was clear that the differences between the two sides were irreconcilable, and both prepared for war by raising armies. The first battle of the English Civil War occurred in October 1642 between the armies of the king and parliament at Edgehill. The war raged, and Charles was taken into captivity in 1647. He was charged with treason, and in 1649 convicted by a court created especially for the purposes of that trial, as the existing courts considered Charles' indictment to be illegal. He was executed on 30 January 1649.

Charles' trial and execution had been made possible by a purge of Royalists from the parliament just a month earlier. At the time of his death, the parliamentary numbers that remained—the Rump Parliament—assumed all executive authority and power. Between 1649 and the installation of Charles' son, Charles II, to the English throne, England was ruled not as a monarchy but as a republic—for the only time in English history.

This was a time of intellectual ferment, when radical ideas such as universal male suffrage and liberal ideas of freedom of speech were being aired. It was a period in which the two great sides of politics—Whigs and Tories—developed. 'Whig' was originally a term of abuse used against those who supported parliament and the people against the king. The word was a derivation of a Scottish word, 'whiggamor', meaning someone who herded cattle. Tories were more likely to support the king and a conservative position. The description also originated as an insult, from the Irish word for a bandit, 'toraighe'. Over centuries the Whigs would evolve into the Liberal and then parts of the Labour Party in England, while the Tories would become the Conservative Party.

After a few years of confusion, during which the country was governed by the Rump Parliament, executive power was acquired by one of the parliament's military commanders, Oliver Cromwell.

The rule of Cromwell was quasi-dictatorial, characterised by a form of military rule and a moral and religious sense of governmental purpose. For the first time the English government had a standing army. Political power was concentrated in Cromwell. In the first half of the twentieth century, historians and popular writers would compare the rule of Cromwell to that of Hitler and Mussolini. That view is now regarded as an ahistorical exaggeration. For its time, Cromwell's government was relatively tolerant.

Nevertheless, Cromwell was openly disdainful of some of the icons of English liberty, and first among them was the Magna Carta. In 1654 one London merchant, by the name of George Cony, refused to pay customs duties on imported silk because he argued the duties had not been correctly approved by the parliament. He was imprisoned. Cromwell's Instrument of Government allowed the executive to levy customs duties, yet Cony's lawyer challenged this on the basis of the ancient liberties embodied in the Magna Carta. Depending on whose account we follow, either Cromwell told the court that if it wanted to rely on the Magna Carta, 'they must put on a helmet and troop for it' or he dismissed the document by saying the 'magna farta should not control his actions'. When the presiding judge resigned and was replaced by a Cromwell loyalist, Cony saw the writing on the wall, paid the duties, and was released from prison.

Cromwell had been offered, and declined, the title of king halfway through his reign. Nevertheless, he was granted rule for life and when he died in 1658 power transferred to his son, Richard Cromwell. Richard was unable to maintain government. A reconstituted Long Parliament containing those who had been purged in 1648 dissolved itself. A new parliament was formed in 1660 and it asked the son of Charles I to become king. The coronation of Charles II took place in April 1661.

A difficult question for the king and parliament was the issue of whether the prerogatives asserted by parliament in the midst of the Civil War should be allowed to continue. In the end a compromise was reached whereby much of the Long Parliament's legislation was maintained, while Charles II gained enough of his father's powers for it to look as if the monarchy had been genuinely restored. Parliament gained authority over customs duties and the regulation of overseas trade. The restoration agreement also reiterated Cromwell's decision to abolish knights' tenure for land holding. This made many of the Magna Carta's chapters an effective dead letter, formally ending the feudal economic system and the charter's regulation of that system. Paradoxically, this only enhanced the iconic status of the Magna Carta as a protector of English liberties.

It was the controversy over the succession plans of Charles II—his successor was presumed to be his Catholic brother James—that inspired the writing of John Locke's *Two Treatises of Government*, the seminal liberal text on individual liberties and property rights. Locke's ideas of natural rights were distinct from the ancient constitution espoused by Edward Coke. While Coke believed English liberties were rooted in English tradition, Locke argued rights existed in a state of nature, were inherent to personhood, universal, and not dependent on any historical or statutory foundation. Despite these philosophical differences, the two ideas coexisted to inform later constitutional developments in England and the United States. Hence the American founders could describe individual rights as inalienable and self-evident, yet still derive their legal and constitutional tradition from the ancient English liberties embodied in King John's charter.

On the death of Charles II in 1685, James became king. He was the first Catholic monarch since Mary a century earlier. James II's reign was brief. In 1688 a parliament invited William of Orange to rule with his wife Mary, James' daughter. This was an enormous symbolic step that forever established parliament's supremacy over the monarchy. This Glorious Revolution, named as such by propagandists for its supposed bloodlessness, was a wholesale revision of the English constitution.

This new constitutional arrangement—whereby effectively parliament chose the king—unified the claims about the ancient liberties embodied in the constitution with the new ideas of natural rights. In January 1689 John Locke received a famous letter from one of his correspondents, Lady Mordaunt, imploring him to expound on his radical ideas about natural rights and individual sovereignty. She wrote that James II 'whent out: Lyke a farding candele: and has given us by convension an occasion not of amending the government: but of melting itt downe and make all new'. Yet Locke was not in favour of 'melting' down government and starting again. He argued that simply that the 'ancient constitution' should be restored as 'the best possibly that ever was if taken and put togeather all of a piece in its orginall constitution.' In the context of late seventeenth century politics Locke's hopes for a new liberal political order rested on the evolution of the ideas of the Magna Carta.

The constitutional pinnacle of the Glorious Revolution was the *Bill of Rights*, an Act of Parliament passed in 1689. It reiterated the claims parliament made for itself, such as parliament being the supreme legislative authority and the prohibition on the king suspending or repealing laws without parliamentary approvals. It also declared there was to be no standing army, parliaments were be held frequently, and parliamentarians had the freedom to criticise the king. And of course, the *Bill of Rights* included an echo of that great principle that had been fought for since 1215:

> That levying money for or to the use of the Crown by pretence of prerogative, without grant of Parliament, for longer time, or in other manner than the same is or shall be granted, is illegal.

CONCLUSION

W**hy the Magna Carta? The question of what is special about the Magna Carta goes to the heart of any discussion about the enduring significance of what happened at Runnymede in June 1215. The Magna Carta was not unique in European history. In the Middle Ages it was quite common for monarchs to issue charters not very different from the Magna Carta. The best-known example is the Golden Bull of 1222, forced on King Andrew II of Hungary by disaffected nobles. Under its terms, nobles could legally disobey a king who was not acting according to the law.

But as the political scientist Francis Fukuyama has noted, the Golden Bull didn't become the foundation for a political system in Hungary, as the Magna Carta did in England. From the fourteenth century onwards, democracy was developing in England while royal absolutism was taking hold in the rest of Europe. Fukuyama asks, 'Why didn't England end up like Hungary?' He gives two answers.

The first lies in the fact that England had a relatively centralised and well-regarded government. The English preferred to reform their administration rather than revolutionise it. The other reason England developed as it did, according to Fukuyama, was because its society was mobile and open to non-elites. Why England is different has been speculated upon for centuries. Montesquieu visiting England in 1729 wrote 'I am here in a country which hardly resembles the rest of Europe.' In his *Spirit of the Laws*, Montesquieu noted that England was a commercial nation because they were a 'free people'. When Napoleon said 'England is a nation of shopkeepers' he actually didn't mean it as an insult. He recognised England's wealth was a product of its trade, not its population or the extent of its territory.

In his book *The Origins of English Individualism*, Alan Macfarlane noted an intriguing difference between English land law in the Middle Ages and land law in other parts of Europe. In England, individuals owned the land, and they could buy and sell land as they wished—all property was purchasable—a premise contrary to law in nearly every other part of the world. In other countries, there was communal ownership of the land and significant restrictions on what could be done with the land. The consequence of this was, for example, that English agriculture became 'individualistic' while French agriculture remained 'communal'. In England decisions about land were made by individuals, not the family or a set of families. The assumption that individuals were free to acquire and dispose of property runs through the whole of the Magna Carta.

The Magna Carta was a compact between the barons—an elite strata of a few dozen people—and King John. The barons' interests were not necessarily aligned with the mass of people below them—the freemen and bonded peasants who ultimately bore the brunt of political and economic oppression. The campaign against John was a tax rebellion waged by a highly privileged class.

A century and a half after the baronial rebellion, England was rocked by another violent tax rebellion. This time the revolt emanated not from the elites, but from the peasantry. In 1381, the peasantry of England rose up against a much-hated poll tax.

The shape of English society in the fourteenth century was different from that of a hundred years earlier. The Black Death had wiped out nearly half the population. In the wake of such devastation the peasantry were economically empowered. Fewer workers led to sharply higher wages. The king and parliament responded by trying to cap wages. Such labour market regulation was predictable and futile. Peasants no longer felt bound to the land, and sought out better opportunities elsewhere.

Economic change led to political struggle. The Peasants' Revolt of 1381 was sparked by the levying of a series of national poll taxes to pay for England's war against France. This was a form of taxation invented by parliament. By spreading the burden of taxation onto every person, rich or poor, who was not a beggar and over the age of fourteen, the wealthy members of parliament were easing the burden of the tax system on themselves. A poll tax was levied in 1377 and 1379. A third poll tax was levied in 1380. Widespread evasion of this third tax led to the establishment of oppressive commissioners to enforce the tax. The rebellion started in May 1381. Led by Wat Tyler, it spread rapidly across England. A peasant's army entered London, ransacking government buildings. In a confrontation with the fourteen-year-old Richard II and his army at Smithfield, Tyler was killed. The rebellion ended and in its aftermath more than 1,500 rebels were executed.

The Peasants' Revolt was not solely in response to the poll tax. Among the demands the peasants made was the abolition of serfdom—that is, the end of the feudal system—and a reflection of the strikingly different economic circumstances that England had found itself in after the ravages of the Black Death. The rebellion ended in failure, yet parliament had learned an important lesson. The poll tax was removed from the armoury of English taxation until it was revived in the seventeenth century. When a poll tax was levied under the government of Margaret Thatcher in 1989, it led to demonstrations and riots, and ultimately Thatcher's resignation.

Nevertheless, the Peasants' Revolt did not resonate through history in the same way that the barons' rebellion of 1215 did. Perhaps, had the rebellion been successful, there would today be Wat Tyler's shadow in the English constitutional settlement. The Peasants' Revolt has long been an interest and focus of economic and Marxist historians, while political historians have focused on the Magna Carta.

King John was the quintessential Bad King. His reputation is such that no other future monarch was named John. There were a number of Henrys, Richards, and Edwards, but he was the first and last John. In the centuries after Runnymede, anyone seeking a precedent to use against a bad king or a bad government had to look no further than the Magna Carta. If the Magna Carta had not existed, something else would have had to take its place. The reissue of the Magna Carta in 1216 gave the document a status beyond that of a mere peace treaty that, in any case, was repudiated within three months of it being agreed. The wars of John, Henry III, and Edward I against France placed huge financial burdens on all of the English population, and especially the wealthy. It was to be expected that hard-pressed taxpayers would seek some protection against the increasing extractions of the

Crown. Tax was the cause of all the great constitutional struggles of English history. It was inevitable that first great dispute about tax would become iconic.

The Magna Carta is in places alternately vague and specific. Sir James Holt, author of a seminal 1965 book on the Magna Carta, put it nicely:

> Sometimes Magna Carta stated law. Sometimes it stated what its supporters hoped would become law. Sometimes it stated what they pretended was law. As a party manifesto it made a party case with scant regard for fact or existing practice.

At the same time, the Magna Carta was remarkably precise, such as when it specified the relief to be paid for a barony at £100. Or when, in Chapter 39, it listed the six things—being taken, imprisoned, disseised, outlawed, or exiled—that could not be imposed on a freeman without the lawful judgment of his peers and by the law of the land. William McKechnie identified this sort of precision as one reason for the long-term success of the Magna Carta:

> Definition is a valuable protection for the weak against the strong; vagueness favours the tyrant who can interpret while he enforces the law. Misty rights were now reduced to a tangible form, and could no longer be broken with impunity.

For McKechnie, the Magna Carta was also a uniquely English document. It was practical, which he thought 'is an English characteristic, and strikes the key-note of almost every great movement for reform which has succeeded in English history.' McKechnie compared the English who have 'occupied lower but surer ground, aiming at practical remedies for actual wrongs' to the French and Americans who founded their liberties 'on a lofty but unstable basis of philosophical theory'.

McKechnie was following Edmund Burke, who had made the same argument about English liberties two hundred years before. In his *Reflections on the Revolution in France*, written in 1790, Burke said the Magna Carta symbolised the 'ancient standing law of the kingdom'. Those who resorted to inventing new rights and new ways of doing things would fail, as Burke thought the French revolutionaries would fail. In contrast, the Magna Carta was not an innovation, and that is why it succeeded.

The Magna Carta matters today not because of its detailed outline of feudal rights and royal limitations—and certainly not because the barons were passionate about the equal rights of the citizenry—but because of the way the charter set the development of democratic liberalism in train. The requirement that taxes could only be levied with the common counsel of the realm was a crack in the heart of absolutist government. Not only was this power over tax a potent bargaining chip over the other activities of the Crown, but it was necessary for the functioning of those activities. The most expensive pastime of the English royalty was waging war. Indeed, it was Angevin foreign policy that brought John's kingship to a crisis. Likewise, Henry III found his reckoning over his foreign policy. Charles I lost the support of parliament within a few years of becoming king because of his wars. The foreign policy of monarchs, financed by taxes, were the vehicle for the scrutiny of the king.

Oppressive taxes require oppressive methods of collection. Taxpayers minimise, avoid, or just outright evade taxes that they are either unable to pay or consider unjust. The iconic *habeas corpus* case of the reign of Charles I—the Five Knights case—was about a refusal to pay tax. Likewise, so much of King John's brutality and arbitrary rule was a consequence of his attempt to soak up as much wealth from English lands as possible. Imposing harsh fines and charges on traditional feudal rights was John's basic fiscal strategy. Both the burden of taxation and the methods by which he enforced the taxes were brutal. And more importantly, the taxpayers felt that he was violating unwritten norms that governed the relationship between themselves and the state.

Indeed, the story of the Magna Carta tells us a great deal about this financial relationship. It matters how tax revenues are spent. The U.S. Supreme Court Justice Oliver Wendell Holmes famously said that 'taxes are what we pay for civilized society'. But John, Henry III, and Charles I were not buying a civilised society. John and Henry III were trying to buy back an empire, and Charles I was playing geopolitics. Royal adventures may have been important to the monarchs but it was the people, not the monarchs themselves, who were asked to finance the burden.

The thirteenth century fiscal constitution embodied in the Magna Carta differs from our own in many ways. Two in particular are important to highlight.

First, our modern society is democratic. The society of King John was not. Democracy offers taxpayers a suggestion that all taxation is consensual; that the people's representatives have approved the collection of tax. Yet while modern democracies have universal suffrage, this doesn't mean that the actions of democratic governments always reflect the will of the people. Neither does it mean that taxpayers always feel their interests are being represented. There are too many problems with political incentives, voting arrangements, and weaknesses in accountability to claim that the will of the democratic state is the will of the people. Governments, whether democratic or autocratic, are constrained in what they can tax and how much tax they can levy. Tax resistance, then and now, manifests itself first as tax avoidance— then tax evasion. Ultimately any government that levies taxes too far above the expectations of its citizens will face resistance. Democratic mechanisms of representation help close the gap between expectations and consent but they do not eliminate it.

The second distinction between the world of King John and ours is the institutional structure of tax. Taxes today are levied on a permanent basis and across a broad base. The impositions that the medieval English found so grating were those imposed arbitrarily and sporadically. They were used for specific purposes—the raising of Richard's ransom and the creation of an army to retake Normandy. There was a tight conceptual relationship between the tax that was raised and the purposes for which it was raised. Few barons were interested in reclaiming John's patrimony over the continent and they resented having to finance its reconquest. There will always be taxpayers who disagree with the purposes for which taxes are raised. But John's purposes were so radically distant from the wishes of his barons that it sparked a civil war.

Tax is everywhere and at all times controversial. The plucked goose is always going to hiss. Thus the historian Charles Adams writes:

> Taxes are a powerful mover of people, more than governments either care to admit or realize. Angry taxpayers can be a lethal threat to a government that institutes oppressive taxation. Taxpayers instinctively rebel: the first warning phase of rebellion is rampant tax evasion and flight to avoid tax; the second phase produces riots; and the third phase is violence. Life ultimately can be catastrophic for any government that pushes its taxpayers too far.

Over centuries, the Magna Carta became both less than the sum of its parts, and much more. The specific issues of thirteenth century taxation fell away. The rules on scutage, tallage, and wardship became anachronisms as England became a capitalist economy. Yet the principles embodied in the Magna Carta did not disappear. They were fought over for the next eight centuries.

Some tax rebellions end in brutal suppression. Others result in civil war, revolution, and wholesale regime change. Yet what happened at Runnymede stands apart from other tax rebellions. A revolt of an unrepresentative elite forged liberal democracy. And now, the fundamental basis of liberal democracy is this: government must gain the consent of its citizens to take taxes from them.

THE 1215 MAGNA CARTA IN ENGLISH

The following translation is from William Sharp McKechnie, *Magna Carta: A Commentary on the Great Charter of King John, with an Historical Introduction* (1914).

John, by the grace of God, king of England, lord of Ireland, duke of Normandy and Aquitaine, and count of Anjou, to the archbishops, bishops, abbots, earls, barons, justiciars, foresters, sheriffs, stewards, servants, and to all his bailiffs and liege subjects, greeting. Know that, having regard to God and for the salvation of our souls, and those of all our ancestors and heirs, and unto the honour of God and the advancement of holy Church, and for the reform of our realm, we have granted as underwritten, by advice of our venerable fathers, Stephen, archbishop of Canterbury, primate of all England and cardinal of the holy Roman Church, Henry archbishop of Dublin, William of

London, Peter of Winchester, Jocelyn of Bath and Glastonbury, Hugh of Lincoln, Walter of Worcester, William of Coventry, Benedict of Rochester, bishops; of master Pandulf, subdeacon and member of the household of our lord the Pope, of brother Aymeric (master of the Knights of the Temple in England), and of the illustrious men William Marshal, earl of Pembroke, William, earl of Salisbury, William, earl Warenne, William, earl of Arundel, Alan of Galloway (constable of Scotland), Waren Fitz Gerald, Peter Fitz Herbert, Hubert de Burgh (seneschal of Poitou), Hugh de Neville, Matthew Fitz Herbert, Thomas Basset, Alan Basset, Philip d'Aubigny, Robert of Roppesley, John Marshal, John Fitz Hugh, and others, our liegemen.

Chapter 1: In the first place we have granted to God, and by this our present charter confirmed for us and our heirs for ever that the English church shall be free, and shall have her rights entire, and her liberties inviolate; and we will that it be thus observed; which is apparent from this that the freedom of elections, which is reckoned most important and very essential to the English church, we, of our pure and unconstrained will, did grant, and did by our charter confirm and did obtain the ratification of the same from our lord, Pope Innocent III, before the quarrel arose between us and our barons: and this we will observe, and our will is that it be observed in good faith by our heirs for ever. We have also granted to all freemen of our kingdom, for us and our heirs forever, all the underwritten liberties, to be had and held by them and their heirs, of us and our heirs forever.

Chapter 2: If any of our earls or barons, or others holding of us in chief by military service shall have died, and at the time of his death his heir shall be full of age and owe 'relief' he shall have his inheritance on payment of the ancient relief, namely the heir or heirs of an earl, £100 for a whole earl's barony; the heir or heirs of a baron, £100 for a whole barony; the heir or heirs of a knight, 100s. at most for a whole knight's fee; and whoever owes less let him give less, according to the ancient custom of fiefs.

Chapter 3: If, however, the heir of any one of the aforesaid has been under age and in wardship, let him have his inheritance without relief and without fine when he comes of age.

Chapter 4: The guardian of the land of an heir who is thus under age, shall take from the land of the heir nothing but reasonable produce, reasonable customs, and reasonable services, and that without destruction or waste of men or goods; and if we have committed the wardship of the lands of any such minor to the sheriff, or to any other who is responsible to us for its issues, and he has made destruction or waste of what he holds in wardship, we will take of him amends, and the land shall be committed to two lawful and discreet men of that fee, who shall be responsible for the issues to us or to him to whom we shall assign them; and if we have given or sold the wardship of any such land to anyone and he has therein made destruction or waste, he shall lose that wardship, and it shall be transferred to two lawful and discreet men of that fief, who shall be responsible to us in like manner as aforesaid.

Chapter 5: The guardian, moreover, so long as he has the wardship of the land, shall keep up the houses, parks, fishponds, stanks, mills, and other things pertaining to the land, out of the issues of the same land; and he shall restore to the heir, when he has come to full age, all his land, stocked with ploughs and 'wainage', according as the season of husbandry shall require, and the issues of the land can reasonably bear.

Chapter 6: Heirs shall be married without disparagement, yet so that before the marriage takes place the nearest in blood to that heir shall have notice.

Chapter 7: A widow, after the death of her husband, shall forthwith and without difficulty have her marriage portion and inheritance; nor shall she give anything for her dower, or for her marriage portion, or for the inheritance which her husband and she held on the day of the death of that husband; and she may remain in the house of her husband for forty days after his death, within which time her dower shall be assigned to her.

Chapter 8: No widow shall be compelled to marry, so long as she prefers to live without a husband; provided always that she gives security not to marry without our consent, if she holds of us, or without the consent of the lord of whom she holds, if she holds of another.

Chapter 9: Neither we nor our bailiffs shall seize any land or rent for any debt, so long as the chattels of the debtor are sufficient to repay the debt; nor shall the sureties of the debtor be distrained so long as the principal debtor is able to satisfy the debt; and if the principal debtor shall fail to pay the debt, having nothing wherewith to pay it, then the sureties shall answer for the debt; and let them have the lands and rents of the debtor, if they desire them, until they are indemnified for the debt which they have paid for him, unless the principal debtor can show proof that he is discharged thereof as against the said sureties.

Chapter 10: If one who has borrowed from the Jews any sum, great or small, die before that loan be repaid, the debt shall not bear interest while the heir is under age, of whomsoever he may hold; and if the debt fall into our hands, we will not take anything except the principal sum contained in the bond.

Chapter 11: And if anyone die indebted to the Jews, his wife shall have her dower and pay nothing of that debt; and if any children of the deceased are left under age, necessaries shall be provided for them in keeping with the holding of the deceased; and out of the residue the debt shall be paid, reserving, however, service due to feudal lords; in like manner let it be done touching debts due to others than Jews.

Chapter 12: No scutage nor aid shall be imposed on our kingdom, unless by common counsel of our kingdom, except for ransoming our person, for making our eldest son a knight, and for once marrying our eldest daughter; and for these there shall not be levied more than a reasonable aid. In like manner it shall be done concerning aids from the city of London.

Chapter 13: And the city of London shall have all its ancient liberties and free customs, as well by land as by water; furthermore, we decree and grant that all other cities, boroughs, towns, and ports shall have all their liberties and free customs.

Chapter 14: And for obtaining the common counsel of the kingdom anent the assessing of an aid (except in the three cases aforesaid) or of a scutage, we will cause to be summoned the archbishops, bishops, abbots, earls, and greater barons, severally by our letters; and we will moreover cause to be summoned generally, through our sheriffs and bailiffs, all others who hold of us in chief, for a fixed date, namely, after the expiry of at least forty days, and at a fixed place; and in all letters of such summons we will specify the reason of the summons. And when the summons has thus been made, the business shall proceed on the day appointed, according to the counsel of such as are present, although not all who were summoned have come.

Chapter 15: We will not for the future grant to any one licence to take an aid from his own free tenants, except to ransom his body, to make his eldest son a knight, and once to marry his eldest daughter; and on each of these occasions there shall be levied only a reasonable aid.

Chapter 16: No one shall be distrained for performance of greater service for a knight's fee, or for any other free tenement, than is due therefrom.

Chapter 17: Common pleas shall not follow our court, but shall be held in some fixed place.

Chapter 18: Inquests of *novel disseisin*, of *mort d'ancestor,* and of *darrein presentment*, shall not be held elsewhere than in their own county–courts, and that in manner following—We, or, if we should be out of the realm, our chief justiciar, will send two justiciars through every county four times a year, who shall, along with four knights of the county chosen by the county, hold the said assizes in the county court, on the day and in the place of meeting of that court.

Chapter 19: And if any of the said assizes cannot be taken on the day of the county court, let there remain of the knights and freeholders, who were present at the county court on that day, as many as may be required for the efficient making of judgments, according as the business be more or less.

Chapter 20: A freeman shall not be amerced for a slight offence, except in accordance with the degree of the offence; and for a grave offence he shall be amerced in accordance with the gravity of the offence, yet saving always his 'contenement'; and a merchant in the same way, saving his 'merchandise'; and a villein shall be amerced in the same way, saving his 'wainage'—if they have fallen into our mercy: and none of the aforesaid amercements shall be imposed except by the oath of honest men of the neighbourhood.

Chapter 21: Earls and barons shall not be amerced except through their peers, and only in accordance with the degree of the offence.

Chapter 22: A clerk shall not be amerced in respect of his lay holding except after the manner of the others aforesaid; further, he shall not be amerced in accordance with the extent of his ecclesiastical benefice.

Chapter 23: No village or individual shall be compelled to make bridges at river banks, except those who from of old were legally bound to do so.

Chapter 24: No sheriff, constable, coroners, or others of our bailiffs, shall hold pleas of our Crown.

Chapter 25: All counties, hundreds, wapentakes, and trithings (except our demesne manors) shall remain at the old rents, and without any additional payment.

Chapter 26: If any one holding of us a lay fief shall die, and our sheriff or bailiff shall exhibit our letters patent of summons for a debt which the deceased owed to us, it shall be lawful for our sheriff or bailiff to attach and catalogue chattels of the deceased, found upon the lay fief, to the value of that debt, at the sight of law-worthy men, provided always that nothing whatever be thence removed until the debt which is evident shall be fully paid to us; and the residue shall be left to the executors to fulfil the will of the deceased; and if there be nothing due from him to us, all the chattels shall go to the deceased, saving to his wife and children their reasonable shares.

Chapter 27: If any freeman shall die intestate, his chattels shall be distributed by the hands of his nearest kinsfolk and friends, under supervision of the church, saving to every one the debts which the deceased owed to him.

Chapter 28: No constable or other bailiff of ours shall take corn or other provisions from any one without immediately tendering money therefor, unless he can have postponement thereof by permission of the seller.

Chapter 29: No constable shall compel any knight to give money in lieu of castle-guard, when he is willing to perform it in his own person, or (if he himself cannot do it from any reasonable cause) then by another responsible man. Further, if we have led or sent him upon military service, he shall be relieved from guard in proportion to the time during which he has been on service because of us.

Chapter 30: No sheriff or bailiff of ours, or other person, shall take the horses or carts of any freeman for transport duty, against the will of the said freeman.

Chapter 31: Neither we nor our bailiffs shall take, for our castles or for any other work of ours, wood which is not ours, against the will of the owner of that wood.

Chapter 32: We will not retain beyond one year and one day, the lands of those who have been convicted of felony, and the lands shall thereafter be handed over to the lords of the fiefs.

Chapter 33: All kydells for the future shall be removed altogether from Thames and Medway, and throughout all England, except upon the sea shore.

Chapter 34: The writ which is called *praecipe* shall not for the future be issued to anyone, regarding any tenement whereby a freeman may lose his court.

Chapter 35: Let there be one measure of wine throughout our whole realm; and one measure of ale; and one measure of corn, to wit, 'the London quarter'; and one width of cloth (whether dyed, or russet, or 'halberget'), to wit, two ells within the selvedges; of weights also let it be as of measures.

Chapter 36: Nothing in future shall be given or taken for a writ of inquisition of life or limbs, but freely it shall be granted, and never denied.

Chapter 37: If anyone holds of us by fee-farm, by socage, or by burgage, and holds also land of another lord by knight's service, we will not (by reason of that fee-farm, socage, or burgage) have the wardship of the heir, or of such land of his as is of the fief of that other; nor shall we have wardship of that fee-farm, socage, or burgage, unless such fee-farm owes knight's service. We will not by reason of any small serjeanty which anyone may hold of us by the service of rendering to us knives, arrows, or the like, have wardship of his heir or of the land which he holds of another lord by knight's service.

Chapter 38: No bailiff for the future shall, upon his own unsupported complaint, put anyone to his 'law,' without credible witnesses brought for this purpose.

Chapter 39: No freeman shall be taken or [and] imprisoned or disseised or exiled or in any way destroyed, nor will we go upon him nor send upon him, except by the lawful judgment of his peers or [and] by the law of the land.

Chapter 40: To no one will we sell, to no one will we refuse or delay, right or justice.

Chapter 41: All merchants shall have safe and secure exit from

England, and entry to England, with the right to tarry there and to move about as well by land as by water, for buying and selling by the ancient and right customs, quit from all evil tolls, except (in time of war) such merchants as are of the land at war with us. And if such are found in our land at the beginning of the war, they shall be detained, without injury to their bodies or goods, until information be received by us, or by our chief justiciar, how the merchants of our land found in the land at war with us are treated; and if our men are safe there, the others shall be safe in our land.

Chapter 42: It shall be lawful in future for any one (excepting always those imprisoned or outlawed in accordance with the law of the kingdom, and natives of any country at war with us, and merchants, who shall be treated as is above provided) to leave our kingdom and to return, safe and secure by land and water, except for a short period in time of war, on grounds of public policy— reserving always the allegiance due to us.

Chapter 43: If anyone holding of some escheat (such as the honour of Wallingford, Nottingham, Boulogne, Lancaster, or of other escheats which are in our hands and are baronies) shall die, his heir shall give no other relief, and perform no other service to us than he would have done to the baron, if that barony had been in the baron's hand; and we shall hold it in the same manner in which the baron held it.

Chapter 44: Men who dwell without the forest need not henceforth come before our justiciars of the forest upon a general summons, except those who are impleaded, or who have become sureties for any person or persons attached for forest offences.

Chapter 45: We will appoint as justices, constables, sheriffs, or bailiffs only such as know the law of the realm and mean to observe it well.

Chapter 46: All barons who have founded abbeys, concerning which they hold charters from the kings of England, or of which they have long-continued possession, shall have the wardship of them, when vacant, as they ought to have.

Chapter 47: All forests that have been made such in our time shall forthwith be disafforested; and a similar course shall be followed with regard to river-banks that have been placed 'in defence' by us in our time.

Chapter 48: All evil customs connected with forests and warrens, foresters and warreners, sheriffs and their officers, river–banks and their wardens, shall immediately be inquired into in each county by twelve sworn knights of the same county chosen by the honest men of the same county, and shall, within forty days of the said inquest, be utterly abolished, so as never to be restored, provided always that we previously have intimation thereof, or our justiciar, if we should not be in England.

Chapter 49: We will immediately restore all hostages and charters delivered to us by Englishmen, as sureties of the peace or of faithful service.

Chapter 50: We will entirely remove from their bailiwicks, the relations of Gerard of Athée (so that in future they shall have no bailiwick in England); namely, Engelard of Cigogné, Peter, Guy, and Andrew of Chanceaux, Guy of Cigogné, Geoffrey of Martigny with his brothers, Philip Mark with his brothers and his nephew Geoffrey, and the whole brood of the same.

Chapter 51: As soon as peace is restored, we will banish from the kingdom all foreign-born knights, cross-bowmen, serjeants, and mercenary soldiers, who have come with horses and arms to the kingdom's hurt.

Chapter 52: If any one has been dispossessed or removed by us, without the legal judgment of his peers, from his lands, castles, franchises, or from his right, we will immediately restore them to him; and if a dispute arise over this, then let it be decided by the five-and-twenty barons of whom mention is made below in the clause for securing the peace. Moreover, for all those possessions, from which any one has, without the lawful judgment of his peers, been disseised or removed, by our father, King Henry, or by our brother, King Richard, and which we retain in our hand (or which are possessed by others, to whom we are bound to warrant them) we shall have respite until the usual term of crusaders; excepting those things about which a plea has been raised, or an inquest made by our order, before our taking of the cross; but as soon as we return from our expedition (or if perchance we desist from the expedition) we will immediately grant full justice therein.

Chapter 53: We shall have, moreover, the same respite and in the same manner in rendering justice concerning the disafforestation or retention of those forests which Henry our father and Richard our brother afforested, and concerning the wardship of lands which are of the fief of another (namely, such wardships as we have hitherto had by reason of a fief which anyone held of us by knight's service), and concerning abbeys founded on other fiefs than our own, in which the lord of the fee claims to have right; and when we have returned, or if we desist from our expedition, we will immediately grant full justice to all who complain of such things.

Chapter 54: No one shall be arrested or imprisoned upon the appeal of a woman, for the death of any other than her husband.

Chapter 55: All fines made with us unjustly and against the law of the land, and all amercements imposed unjustly and against the law of the land, shall be entirely remitted, or else it shall be done concerning them according to the decision of the five-and-twenty barons of whom mention is made below in the clause for securing the peace, or according to the judgment of the majority of the same, along with the aforesaid Stephen, archbishop of Canterbury, if he can be present, and such others as he may wish to bring with him for this purpose, and if he cannot be present the business shall nevertheless proceed without him, provided always that if any one or more of the aforesaid five-and-twenty barons are in a similar suit, they shall be removed as far as concerns this particular judgment, others being substituted in their places after having been selected by the rest of the same five-and-twenty for this purpose only, and after having been sworn.

Chapter 56: If we have disseised or removed Welshmen from lands or liberties, or other things, without the legal judgment of their peers in England or in Wales, they shall be immediately restored to them; and if a dispute arise over this, then let it be decided in the marches by the judgment of their peers; for tenements in England according to the law of England, for tenements in Wales according to the law of Wales, and for tenements in the marches according to the law of the marches. Welshmen shall do the same to us and ours.

Chapter 57: Further, for all those possessions from which any Welshman has, without the lawful judgment of his peers, been disseised or removed by King Henry our father, or King Richard our brother, and which we retain in our hand (or which are possessed by others, to whom we are bound to warrant them) we shall have respite until the usual term of crusaders; excepting those things about which a plea has been raised or an inquest made by our order before we took the cross; but as soon as we return, (or if perchance we desist from our expedition), we will immediately grant full justice in accordance with the laws of the Welsh and in relation to the foresaid regions.

Chapter 58: We will immediately give up the son of Llywelyn and all the hostages of Wales, and the charters delivered to us as security for the peace.

Chapter 59: We will do towards Alexander, King of Scots, concerning the return of his sisters and his hostages, and concerning his franchises, and his right, in the same manner as we shall do towards our other barons of England, unless it ought to be otherwise according to the charters which we hold from William his father, formerly King of Scots; and this shall be according to the judgment of his peers in our court.

Chapter 60: Moreover, all these aforesaid customs and liberties, the observance of which we have granted in our kingdom as far as pertains to us towards our men, shall be observed by all of our kingdom, as well clergy as laymen, as far as pertains to them towards their men.

Chapter 61: Since, moreover, for God and the amendment of our kingdom and for the better allaying of the quarrel that has arisen between us and our barons, we have granted all these concessions, desirous that they should enjoy them in complete and firm endurance for ever, we give and grant to them the under-written security, namely, that the barons choose five-and-twenty barons of the kingdom, whomsoever they will, who shall be bound with all their might, to observe and hold, and cause to be observed, the peace and liberties we have granted and confirmed to them by this our present Charter, so that if we, or our justiciar, or our bailiffs or any one of our officers, shall in anything be at fault toward anyone, or shall have broken any one of the articles of the peace or of this security, and the offence be notified to four barons of the foresaid five-and-twenty, the said four barons shall repair to us (or our justiciar, if we are out of the realm) and, laying the transgression before us, petition to have that transgression redressed without delay. And if we shall not have corrected the transgression (or, in the event of our being out of the realm, if our justiciar shall not have corrected it) within forty days, reckoning from the time it has been intimated to us (or to our justiciar, if we should be out of the realm), the four barons aforesaid shall refer that matter to the rest of the five-and-twenty barons, and those five-and-twenty barons shall, together with the community of the whole land, distrain and distress us in all possible ways, namely, by seizing our castles, lands, possessions, and in any other way they can, until redress has been obtained as they deem fit, saving harmless our own person, and the persons of our queen and children; and when redress has been obtained, they shall resume their old relations towards us. And let whoever in the country desires it, swear to obey the orders of the said five-and-twenty barons for the execution of all the aforesaid matters, and along with them, to molest us to the utmost of his power; and we publicly and freely grant leave to every one who wishes to swear, and we shall never forbid anyone to swear. All those, moreover, in the land who of themselves and of their own accord are unwilling to swear to the twenty-five to help them in constraining and molesting us, we shall by our command com-pel the same to swear to the effect foresaid. And if any one of the five-and-twenty barons shall have died or departed from the land, or be incapacitated in any other manner which would prevent the foresaid provisions being carried out, those of the said twenty-five barons who are left shall choose another in his place according to their own judgment, and he shall be sworn in the same way as the others. Further, in all matters, the execution of which is intrusted to these twenty-five barons, if perchance these twenty-five are present and disagree about anything, or if some of them, after being summoned, are unwilling or unable to be present, that which the majority of those present ordain or command shall be held as fixed and established, exactly as if the whole twenty-five had concurred in this; and the said twenty-five shall swear that they will faithfully observe all that is aforesaid, and cause it to be observed with all their might. And we shall procure nothing from anyone, directly or indirectly, whereby any part of these concessions and liberties might be revoked or diminished; and if any such thing has been procured, let it be void and null, and we shall never use it personally or by another.

Chapter 62: And all the ill-will, hatreds, and bitterness that have arisen between us and our men, clergy and lay, from the date of the quarrel, we have completely remitted and pardoned to everyone. Moreover, all trespasses occasioned by the said quarrel, from Easter in the sixteenth year of our reign till the restoration of peace, we have fully remitted to all, both clergy and laymen, and completely forgiven, as far as pertains to us. And, on this head, we have caused to be made for them letters testimonial patent of the lord Stephen, archbishop of Canterbury, of the lord Henry, archbishop of Dublin, of the bishops aforesaid, and of Master Pandulf as touching this security and the concessions aforesaid.

Chapter 63: Wherefore it is our will, and we firmly enjoin, that the English Church be free, and that the men in our kingdom have and hold all the aforesaid liberties, rights, and concessions, well and peaceably, freely and quietly, fully and wholly, for themselves and their heirs, of us and our heirs, in all respects and in all places for ever, as is aforesaid. An oath, moreover, has been taken, as

well on our part as on the part of the barons, that all these conditions aforesaid shall be kept in good faith and without evil intent.
Given under our hand—the above-named and many others being
witnesses—in the meadow which is called Runnymede, between
Windsor and Staines, on the fifteenth day of June, in the seventeenth year of our reign.

References

Introduction

'Prince or State endeavoured': David M. Hart and Ross Kenyon, *Tracts on Liberty by the Levellers and Their Critics*, Vol. 3 (Liberty Fund, 2014), 350.

widely published engraving: Nicholas Vincent, *Magna Carta: A Very Short Introduction* (Oxford University Press, 2012), 116.

'are entitled to the vote': Christabel Pankhurst, 'Suffrage for Women' (8 December 1908).

'arouse my admiration': Nelson Mandela, *The Struggle Is My Life* (International Defence and Aid Fund, 1978), 176.

'**online Magna Carta**': Jemima Kiss, 'An Online Magna Carta: Berners-Lee Calls for Bill of Rights for Web,' *The Guardian*, 12 March 2014.

The Parchment Sealed at Runnymede

'**742 years neglected to erect**': 'American Lawyers Give Magna Carta Shrine,' *The Spokesman-Review*, 29 July 1957.

'**Freedom under law**': 'The Magna Carta Memorial Ceremonies: Runnymede, Sunday Afternoon, July 28,' *ABA Journal* 43, October (1957): 904.

'**judicial assessment of private rights**': Ibid., 906.

'**passing Runnymede**': A. Lascelles and D. Hart-Davis, *King's Counsellor: Abdication and War: The Diaries of Sir Alan Lascelles* (Weidenfeld & Nicolson, 2006), 236.

coronation of Richard I in September 1189: Stephen Church, *King John: England, Magna Carta and the Making of a Tyrant* (Macmillan, 2015), 31.

acts of war against the barons: J.C. Holt, *Magna Carta* (Cambridge University Press, 1992), 248-257.

'**and by the law of the land**': Vincent, *Magna Carta: A Very Short Introduction*.

'**or by the law of the land**': David Carpenter, *Magna Carta* (Penguin, 2015).

'**rest of the population**': Robert Bartlett, *England under the Norman and Angevin Kings, 1075-1225* (Clarendon Press; Oxford University Press, 2000), 207.

was about £73,000: A.L. Poole, *From Domesday Book to Magna Carta 1087-1216* (Oxford University Press, 1993), 2.

who mattered and he knew them all: Peter Ackroyd, *Foundation: The History of England Volume 1* (Pan, Main Market Ed., 2012), 191.

remaining 120 were undeclared: Ibid., 170.

right to control who they were to marry: Church, *King John*, 9.

The Power to Tax

'**simply the power to "take"** ': Geoffrey Brennan and James M. Buchanan, *The Power to Tax: Analytical Foundations of a Fiscal Constitution* (Cambridge University Press, 1980), 8.

'**will become his slaves**': 1 Samuel 8:11-17.

'**man to fear is the tax collector**': Charles Adams, *For Good and Evil: The Impact of Taxes on the Course of Civilization* (Madison Books, 1993), 3.

land, cattle, and other resources: David F. Burg, *A World History of Tax Rebellions: An Encyclopedia of Tax Rebels, Revolts, and Riots from Antiquity to the Present* (Routledge, 2004), 9.

'**there were no tax collectors**': Ibid.

'**except our demesne manors**': Vincent, *Magna Carta*.

history books have recognised: James C. Scott, *Weapons of the Weak: Everyday Forms of Peasant Resistance* (Yale University Press, 1985).

series of ancient tax revolts: Burg, *A World History of Tax Rebellions,* 20-28.

'bequeathed to the plunderers': Tacitus, *Annals,* trans. Arthur Murphy, Vol. 3 (Henry Colburn and Richard Bentley, 1831), 14.31.

'with a tax on our heads!': Richard Hingley and Christina Unwin, *Boudica: Iron Age Warrior Queen* (Hambledon and London, 2005), 54.

'what she had asked': Roger of Wendover, *Flowers of History,* trans. J.A. Giles, Vol. 1 (Henry G. Bohn, 1849), 314-5.

'protest against burdensome taxation': Burg, *A World History of Tax Rebellions,* 78.

'the oppression of a heavy toll': Roger of Wendover, *Flowers of History,* Vol. 1, 319.

'tax-based parliamentary state': David Carpenter, *The Struggle for Mastery: Britain, 1066-1284* (Oxford University Press, 2003), 466.

negotiating to replenish his forces: Stephen Dowell, *A History of Taxation and Taxes in England from the Earliest Times to the Year 1885,* Vol. 1 (Longmans, Green, 1888), 39-40.

to help finance the new Norman rule: Robin R. Mundill, *The King's Jews: Money, Massacre and Exodus in Medieval England* (Continuum, 2010).

'confiscated for the king's use': Marc Morris, *King John: Treachery, Tyranny and the Road to Magna Carta* (Random House, 2015).

economy of collection: Adam Smith, *An Inquiry into the Nature and Causes of the Wealth of Nations* (University of Chicago Press, 1976).

REFERENCES

ENGLAND BEFORE 1215

six of which succeeded: Geoffrey Hindley, *A Brief History of the Magna Carta* (Running Press, 2008).

70 such instances since 1066: Ian Hernon, *Fortress Britain: All the Invasions and Incursions since 1066* (Spellmount, 2013).

'essentially French noblemen': Dan Jones, *Magna Carta: The Making and Legacy of the Great Charter* (Head of Zeus, 2014), 96.

induced mass starvation: Morris, *King John,* 229.

'experienced after 1066': R.W. Southern, 'Presidential Address: Aspects of the European Tradition of Historical Writing: 4. The Sense of the Past,' *Transactions of the Royal Historical Society (Fifth Series),* 23 (1973).

'identify itself firmly as English': Hugh M. Thomas, *The English and the Normans: Ethnic Hostility, Assimilation, and Identity, 1066- C. 1220* (Oxford University Press, 2003), 3-4.

'a union with Satan himself': Winston Churchill, *A History of the English-speaking Peoples,* Vol. 1 (Cassell and Company, 1962), 154.

around 20 kilometres per day: Robert Bartlett, *England under the Norman and Angevin Kings,* 136.

'the customs of the manor': Douglass C. North and Robert Paul Thomas, 'The Rise and Fall of the Manorial System: A Theoretical Model,' *The Journal of Economic History* 31, no. 4 (1971).

'on the part of individuals': Bruno Leoni, *Freedom and the Law* (Van Nostrand, 1961).

binding constraint on behaviour: David J. Bederman, *Custom as a Source of Law* (Cambridge University Press, 2010).

recognisably towns and cities: R. Goddard, *Lordship and Medieval Urbanisation: Coventry, 1043-1355* (Royal Historical Society; Boydell Press, 2004), 1.

'and a payment to the king': Richard H. Britnell, 'The Proliferation of Markets in England, 1200-1349,' *The Economic History Review* 34, no. 2 (1981).

'producers and providers of capital': Phillipp R. Schofield, *Peasant and Community in Medieval England, 1200-1500* (Palgrave-Macmillan, 2003), 155-56.

2.75 per cent per year at most: J.C. Holt, *Magna Carta* (Cambridge University Press, 1992), 34 n17.

to the inflation of the period: Paul Latimer, 'The English Inflation of 1180-1220 Reconsidered,' *Past and Present* 171 (2001): 14.

'economic change than Magna Carta': Paul D.A. Harvey, 'The English Inflation of 1180-1220,' *Past and Present* 61 (1973): 14.

'three times the earlier rates': Ibid. 13.

24 pennies per day by 1220: Nick Barratt, 'The Revenue of King John,' *English Historical Review* 111 (443) (1996): 851.

THE PRICE OF EMPIRE

'unable to do when present': Bartlett, *England under the Norman and Angevin Kings,* 124

'bent to its realisation': W.L. Warren, *King John* (University of California Press, 1978), 1.

kingmaker of the Angevin empire: Elizabeth A.R. Brown, 'Eleanor of Aquitaine: Parent, Queen, and Duchess,' in *Eleanor of*

Aquitaine, Patron and Politician, ed. William W. Kibler (University of Texas Press, 1976).

middle of the twentieth century: Jean Dunbabin, 'Henry II and Louis VII,' in *Henry II: New Interpretations*, ed. Christopher Harper-Bill and Nicholas Vincent (Boydell Press, 2007).

'I have taken vengeance on you': Peter Ackroyd, *Foundation*, 150.

during his decade on the throne: M.T. Clanchy, *England and Its Rulers, 1066-1307* (Blackwell, 2006), 120.

hand over the year's wool clip: Douglas Boyd, *Lionheart: The True Story of England's Crusader King* (The History Press, 2015), 180.

'continually in arrears': Sydney Knox Mitchell, *Studies in Taxation under John and Henry III* (Yale University Press, 1914).

'from every quarter': Gerald of Wales, *Expugnatio Hibernica: The Conquest of Ireland* (Royal Irish Academy, 1978), 211.

such an extraordinary exaction: M. Jurkowski, C.L. Smith, and David Crook, *Lay Taxes in England and Wales 1188-1688* (PRO Publications, 1998), xiii.

between Henry II and John: W.M. Ormrod, 'Royal Finance in Thirteenth Century England,' in *Thirteenth Century England V: Proceedings of the Newcastle Upon Tyne Conference 1993*, ed. Peter R. Coss and Simon D. Lloyd (Boydell & Brewer, 1995), 150.

'seemed only prudent': John Robert Maddicott, *The Origins of the English Parliament, 924-1327* (Oxford University Press, 2010), 120.

'poor to pay everything': Richard de Hoveden, T*he Annals of Roger De Hoveden: Comprising the History of England and of Other Countries of Europe from A.D. 732 to A.D. 1201*, trans. Henry T. Riley (H.G. Bohn, 1853), 388.

'**unusually eloquent … sharp mind**': John McEwan, 'William Fitzosbert and the Crisis of 1196 in London,' *Florilegium* 21 (2004): 22.

52,000 supporters: Bartlett, *England under the Norman and Angevin Kings*, 345.

'**his associates and died**': McEwan, 'William Fitzosbert and the Crisis of 1196 in London,' 26.

The Foulness of John

'**desolated the rest**': William Stubbs, *The Constitutional History of England in Its Origin and Development* (Clarendon Press, 1896).

'**the foulness of John**': Matthew Paris and Richard Vaughan, *Chronicles of Matthew Paris: Monastic Life in the Thirteenth Century* (A. Sutton; St. Martin's Press, 1984).

'**as the pope**': Shakespeare, *King John*, 3.1.73-77.

'**rather than contiguous**': John T. Appleby, *England without Richard, 1189-1199* (G. Bell, 1965), 34.

'**resistance to his attempts**': Ralph V. Turner, *King John* (Longman, 1994), 38.

'**had bad companions**': Ibid., 46.

'**thrown into the river**': Walter de Gray Birch, *A History of Margam Abbey* (Bedford Press, 1897).

'**and calculating about it**': Carpenter, *Magna Carta*.

increasing their financial resources: G.E. Seel, *King John: An Underrated King* (Anthem Press, 2012).

REFERENCES

'indeed of Richard's making': Nick Barratt, 'The Revenues of John and Philip Augustus Revisited,' in *King John: New Interpretations*, ed. S.D. Church (Boydell Press, 1999), 86.

'asset stripping': Nick Barratt, 'Counting the Cost: The Financial Implications of the Loss of Normandy,' in *Thirteenth Century England X*, ed. Michael Prestwich, Richard H. Britnell, and Robert Frame (The Boydell Press, 2005).

to re-establish tariffs: Turner, *King John*.

'that actually raised': Jurkowski, Smith, and Crook, *Lay Taxes in England and Wales*, xx.

'many virtues and few vices': John C. Moore, *Pope Innocent III (1160/61-1216): To Root up and to Plant* (Brill, 2003).

'dangerous for you': Ibid., 173.

'celebrate divine services': Turner, *King John*, 161.

REBELLION

'Magna Carta embodied': Vincent, *Magna Carta*, 36.

'leaders of society': Keith J. Stringer, 'Nobility and Identity in Medieval Britain and Ireland: The De Vescy Family, C. 1120-1314,' in *Britain and Ireland, 900-1300: Insular Responses to Medieval European Change*, ed. Brendan Smith (Cambridge University Press, 1999).

'cautious, even parsimonious': J.C. Holt, *The Northerners: A Study in the Reign of King John* (Clarendon Press, 1961).

'one mind against the king': Walter of Guisborough, *Chronicon Domini Walteri De Hemingburgh*, Vol. 1 (English Historical Society Publications, 1848), 247-49.

'and one of the most powerful': Matthew Strickland, 'Fitzwalter, Robert (D. 1235),' in *Oxford Dictionary of National Biography* (Oxford University Press, 2004).

drove Fitzwalter to rebellion: Kate Norgate, *John Lackland* (Macmillan, 1902), 289-90.

well conceived but for one critical detail: Turner, *King John*.

students of Paris sang and danced: Warren, *King John*.

'landslide' ... support away from the king: Holt, *The Northerners: A Study in the Reign of King John*.

'and confirmed them by his charter': Roger of Wendover, *Flowers of History*, trans. J.A. Giles, 2 vols. (Henry G. Bohn, 1849)

'humane desire': William Sharp McKechnie, *Magna Carta*.

'in respect of the excellency of the matter': Ibid.

'the consent of Parliament': Ibid.

'lies outside his will': Ibid.

interference of the latter in the former: David A. Carpenter, 'Archbishop Langton and Magna Carta: His Contribution, His Doubts and His Hypocrisy,' *The English Historical Review* 126 (522) (2011).

staggering 314 marks: Bartlett, *England under the Norman and Angevin Kings*, 164.

King John's former wife: Holt, *Magna Carta*, 190-91.

REFERENCES

'the Jews themselves': Carpenter, *Magna Carta*, 116.

FROM PEACE TREATY TO CONSTITUTION

'from land to land': David Carpenter, *The Minority of Henry III,* (University of California Press, 1990), 19.

'you will recover your lands': Ibid., 375.

both in its scale and breadth: John Robert Maddicott, *The Origins of the English Parliament, 924-1327* (Oxford University Press, 2010), 235.

MAGNA CARTA AND ENGLISH LIBERTIES

'they are called Gods': Glenn Burgess, 'The Divine Right of Kings Reconsidered,' *English Historical Review* 147 (425) (1992): 837.

'the height of his power': James I et al., *The Workes of the Most High and Mightie Prince, Iames, by the Grace of God King of Great Britaine, France and Ireland, Defender of the Faith* (Robert Barker & John Bill, 1616), 528-31.

'is withal dissolved': George Macaulay Trevelyan, *England under the Stuarts* (Putnam, 1949), 99.

Elizabeth had spent while at war: Ibid., 101.

'king, state and defence of the realm': J.P. Kenyon, *The Stuart Constitution, 1603-1688; Documents and Commentary* (Cambridge University Press, 1966), 42.

'England have sprung': Edward Coke and Steve Sheppard, *The Selected Writings and Speeches of Sir Edward Coke,* Vol. 2, (Liberty Fund, 2003), 848.

sitting of parliament: Ralph V. Turner, *Magna Carta: Through the Ages* (Pearson/Longman, 2003).

'wherein himself doth sit': Alan Cromartie, *The Constitutionalist Revolution: An Essay on the History of England, 1450-1642* (Cambridge University Press, 2006), 207.

'capital and of the nation': Thomas Babington Macaulay, *The History of England from the Accession of James II* (Harper & Brothers, 1856).

The attempt was quickly withdrawn: Robin J.W. Swales, 'The Ship Money Levy of 1628,' *Historical Research* 50 (122) (1977).

'laws of the kingdom?': Turner, *Magna Carta*, 158.

embryonic in the thirteenth century: Anthony Gregory, *The Power of Habeas Corpus in America: From the King's Prerogative to the War on Terror* (Cambridge University Press, 2013).

rule by Charles: Macaulay, *The History of England from the Accession of James II.*

relatively tolerant: Austin Woolrych, 'The Cromwellian Protectorate: A Military Dictatorship?,' *History* 75 (244) (1990).

whose account we follow: Patrick Little and David L. Smith, *Parliaments and Politics During the Cromwellian Protectorate* (Cambridge University Press, 2007), 176.

an effective dead letter: Turner, *Magna Carta.*

'melting itt downe and make all new': Lois G. Schwoerer, 'Locke, Lockean Ideas, and the Glorious Revolution,' *Journal of the History of Ideas* 51 (4) (1990).

'in its orginall constitution': Schwoerer, Ibid.

CONCLUSION

Magna Carta did in England: Francis Fukuyama, *The Origins of Political Order: From Prehuman Times to the French Revolution* (Farrar, Straus and Giroux, 2011).

'Why didn't England end up like Hungary?': Fukuyama, Ibid.

'hardly resembles the rest of Europe': Alan Macfarlane, *The Origins of English Individualism: The Family, Property, and Social Transition* (Cambridge University Press, 1979).

'free people': Montesquieu, *The Spirit of the Laws* (Cambridge University Press, 1989).

'individualistic ... communal': Alan Macfarlane, *The Origins of English Individualism.*

'scant regard for fact or existing practice': Holt, *Magna Carta.*

'be broken with impunity': McKechnie, *Magna Carta,* 122.

'reform which has succeeded in English history': McKechnie, *Magna Carta.*

'lofty but unstable basis of philosophical theory': Ibid., 121.

'ancient standing law of the kingdom': Edmund Burke, *The Works of the Right Honourable Edmund Burke,* Vol. 1 (Wells and Lilly, 1826), 393.

'taxes are what we pay for civilized society': U.S. Supreme Court, *Compania General de Tabacos v. Collector,* 275 U.S. 87 (1927).

'its taxpayers too far': Charles Adams, *For Good and Evil: The Impact of Taxes on the Course of Civilization* (Madison Books, 1993), xxi.

*also from Stockade Books
and the Institute of Public Affairs*

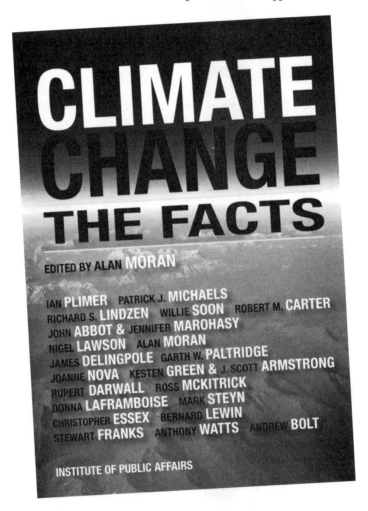

CLIMATE
CHANGE
THE FACTS

EDITED BY ALAN MORAN

IAN PLIMER   PATRICK J. MICHAELS
RICHARD S. LINDZEN   WILLIE SOON   ROBERT M. CARTER
JOHN ABBOT & JENNIFER MAROHASY
NIGEL LAWSON   ALAN MORAN
JAMES DELINGPOLE GARTH W. PALTRIDGE
JOANNE NOVA   KESTEN GREEN & J. SCOTT ARMSTRONG
RUPERT DARWALL   ROSS MCKITRICK
DONNA LAFRAMBOISE   MARK STEYN
CHRISTOPHER ESSEX   BERNARD LEWIN
STEWART FRANKS   ANTHONY WATTS   ANDREW BOLT

INSTITUTE OF PUBLIC AFFAIRS

AMAZON'S NUMBER ONE
CLIMATOLOGY BESTSELLER!